W9-BZO-173

border to border · teen to teen · border to border · teen to teen · border to border

Teens in Iran

by David Seidman

Content Adviser: Faegheh Shirazi, Ph.D.,
Associate Professor, Department of Middle Eastern Studies,
University of Texas at Austin

Reading Adviser: Alexa Sandmann, Ph.D.,
Associate Professor of Literacy,
Kent State University

Compass Point Books ◆ Minneapolis, Minnesota

Compass Point Books
3109 West 50th Street, #115
Minneapolis, MN 55410

Editor: Julie Gassman
Designers: The Design Lab and Jaime Martens
Page Production: Bobbie Nuytten
Photo Researcher: Eric Gohl
Cartographer: XNR Productions, Inc.
Library Consultant: Kathleen Baxter

Art Director: Jaime Martens
Creative Director: Keith Griffin
Editorial Director: Nick Healy
Managing Editor: Catherine Neitge

Author's dedication: To my pal Kate McMains—young in spirit and passionate in politics

Library of Congress Cataloging-in-Publication Data
Seidman, David, 1958–
  Teens in Iran / by David Seidman.
    p. cm.
  ISBN-13: 978-0-7565-3300-7 (library binding)
  ISBN-10: 0-7565-3300-7 (library binding)
  1. Teenagers—Iran—Social conditions—Juvenile literature. 2. Teenagers—Iran—Social
life and customs—Juvenile literature. 3. Iran—Social conditions—21st century—Juve-
nile literature. 4. Iran—Social life and customs—21st century—Juvenile literature. I.
Title.
    HQ799.I62S45 2008
    305.2350955—dc22   2007005411

Visit Compass Point Books on the Internet at *www.compasspointbooks.com*
or e-mail your request to *custserv@compasspointbooks.com*

Table of Contents

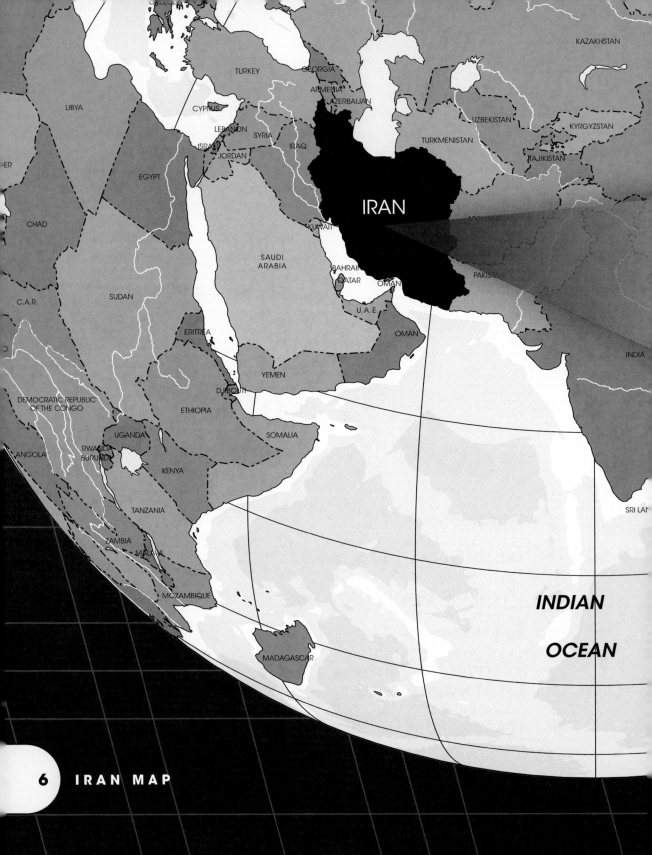

KAZAKHSTAN

TURKEY

GEORGIA

ARMENIA
AZERBAIJAN

LIBYA

CYPRUS

UZBEKISTAN

KYRGYZSTAN

LEBANON

SYRIA

TURKMENISTAN

TAJIKISTAN

ISRAEL

IRAQ

JORDAN

EGYPT

IRAN

AFGHANISTAN

CHAD

KUWAIT

SAUDI
ARABIA

BAHRAIN
QATAR

OMAN

PAKISTAN

C.A.R.

SUDAN

U.A.E.

OMAN

INDIA

ERITREA

YEMEN

DJIBOUTI

DEMOCRATIC REPUBLIC
OF THE CONGO

ETHIOPIA

SOMALIA

ANGOLA

RWANDA
BURUNDI

UGANDA

KENYA

TANZANIA

SRI LAN

ZAMBIA

MALAWI

INDIAN

MOZAMBIQUE

OCEAN

MADAGASCAR

MONGOLIA

NORTH KOREA

SOUTH KOREA

CHINA

Tehran ⭐

NEPAL

BHUTAN

BANGLADESH

MYANMAR

PHILIPPINES

BRUNEI

MALAYSIA

SINGAPORE

INDONESIA

ONE OUT OF EVERY SIX IRANIANS IS A TEENAGER. That's approximately 11 million of them in 2007. They add up to more than the entire population, teens and everyone else, of Sweden, El Salvador, or Hong Kong—or of Israel and Ireland put together. They outnumber their own parents. Iran has more teenagers than people in their 30s or 40s. They number more than the whole Iranian population above age 50.

A crowd that large—in a country that covers more area than France, Spain, and Germany put together—has many different types of teenagers. But they all live under the government's firm Islamic laws. Some of them find guidance and strength in the faith. Others dodge the rules to grab some secret fun, and still others hope to get rid of the restrictions.

All Iranian teenagers, though, deal with school and parents and finding someone to date. In those ways, they are just like teens around the world.

Walking is the most common way for Iranian teens to get to school.

1

Teaching the 18 Million

IT IS SATURDAY MORNING, THE FIRST DAY OF THE WEEK AT SCHOOLS ALL OVER IRAN. Teenagers rush to their classrooms, chatting about what they did over the weekend. But the chatter ends when the teachers step to the front of their classes. In room after room, the students pull out their notebooks and prepare to write down what the teacher says.

They settle in for a day of disciplined education. The teachers lecture, and the students take notes and memorize. They don't spend all of their time sitting, though.

When studying science, for instance, they take a hands-on approach. They may dissect small animals, heat up chemical-filled beakers on Bunsen burners, or examine cells under microscopes. In general, though, the students focus on taking down the teachers' words.

The picture is the same all over the country. The national Ministry of Education makes the decisions for all 18 million students and 113,000 schools (including colleges). Virtually all students obey the same rules, use the same textbooks, and receive instruction in the same way, whether they're in public or private school.

Even the students themselves can seem somewhat similar to each other in appearance. Nearly everyone in Iran is of Middle Eastern or Western Asian descent. The country does have different ethnic groups, but each group tends to live on its own turf. Most Iranian Arabs, for instance, live near the neighboring nation of Saudi Arabia, while the area around Iran's border with Azerbaijan is filled with Iranian Azeris. As a result, the students are nearly all Arab at some schools and mostly Azeri at other schools, and so on.

In addition, schools are separated according to gender. Iranians live by a version of Islam that keeps boys among boys and girls among girls. They rarely mix. Every Iranian high school and middle school is either all male or all female.

Students in all Iranian schools dress alike. All schools require the students to wear uniforms. What's more, Iranian law calls for women and girls to cover up everything but their face and hands with a *hejab*, or veil. Girls schools usually require students' hejabs to be a dark color such as gray, black, or navy blue.

hejab
he-JAAB

Girls and boys play at separate school yards. The majority of students attend gender-specific schools.

Teen Scenes

What do Iranian teenagers do as the day begins? Their routines vary greatly.

Shortly after dawn, a teenage boy fondly pats the family donkey as it pulls a plow through dry soil. The boy lives in a small farming village on the edge of the huge Dasht-e Kavir desert, where he helps his father raise almonds. The boy has been up and working on the farm for hours, but his mind isn't on his work. He looks back at his family's little house of mud and brick. He wonders what will happen tonight when the parents of a girl he has never met will visit his mother and father. If the four adults approve of each other, they will arrange for their children to marry.

Nearly 250 miles (400 kilometers) to the northwest, in northern Tehran's wealthy Tajrish neighborhood, another teenage boy is just waking up. He had been out late at a friend's secret party. It was fun, except for the scary times when the boys and girls thought they heard the police coming. They surely would have arrested them for talking and dancing together. The boy wonders what he'll do after school today. Maybe he'll grab a pizza at the Jaam e-Jam food court. Or he could check out some blogs at an Internet cafe. Or he might buy one of the new Italian shirts at the Tandis shopping mall's Versace clothing store.

A little over 300 miles (just under 500 km) southwest of Tajrish are the villages of western Iran's Zagros Mountains. A 15-year-old girl rises, along with the rest of her family, from morning prayers in their small apartment's living room. As her mother prepares breakfast—boiled eggs, hot tea, feta cheese, and fresh-baked flat bread with butter—the girl adjusts her shapeless black robe to cover everything but her face and hands. It is a typical school morning. She feels fortunate to be going to school. Some rural girls don't make it to high school because the nearest girls school is too far away.

Subjects & Objectives

Iran's schools train their students in subjects that will help them get along in the world. For instance, about 80 percent of the country's teenagers and adults can read and write. That number sets Iran a bit lower than the world average of 82 percent. Iran's literacy rate is still growing, though. Some experts expect Iranians—particularly the young—to rise above the world's average.

Iranian teenagers must learn three languages. Persian, also called Farsi, is the government's official language. Arabic is the language of the Qur'an, Islam's holy book. And English is one of the most widespread world languages, so it joins the curriculum.

Islamic studies and prayers are another part of the curriculum. Islam is more than the religion of most Iranians; it is also the official religion of the government. Through the schools, the government tells teenagers that anyone who opposes Islam or hurts Muslims is an enemy of Iran. Textbooks encourage students to revere both their country and their faith. School officials praise young Iranians who are willing to die for their religion and homeland.

To reinforce this viewpoint, Iranian schools teach the importance of Iran and its history. Iranians have lived in their land since groups of shepherds settled there in around 8000 B.C. Its borders have shifted over the centuries, but today Iran ranks among the world's 20 largest nations. The country lies in western Asia and connects Asia to the Middle East. To its north and east, lie the Caspian Sea and the Asian countries of Afghanistan, Pakistan, and Turkmenistan. The Middle Eastern

School Schedules

The Iranian school year begins on the first day of the Iranian month of Mehr, which usually falls in late September. There's no single, fixed date for the last day of school, but it usually comes in late June.

During the school year, classes start on Saturday and run through Thursday. Iranian schools are closed on Friday, the Islamic Sabbath. Some schools may end early on Thursday afternoon in preparation for the Sabbath.

For middle school or high school, each day begins around 7 or 8 A.M. and ends in the mid-afternoon. In between are about four periods of study, separated by short breaks for rest, snacks, or prayer.

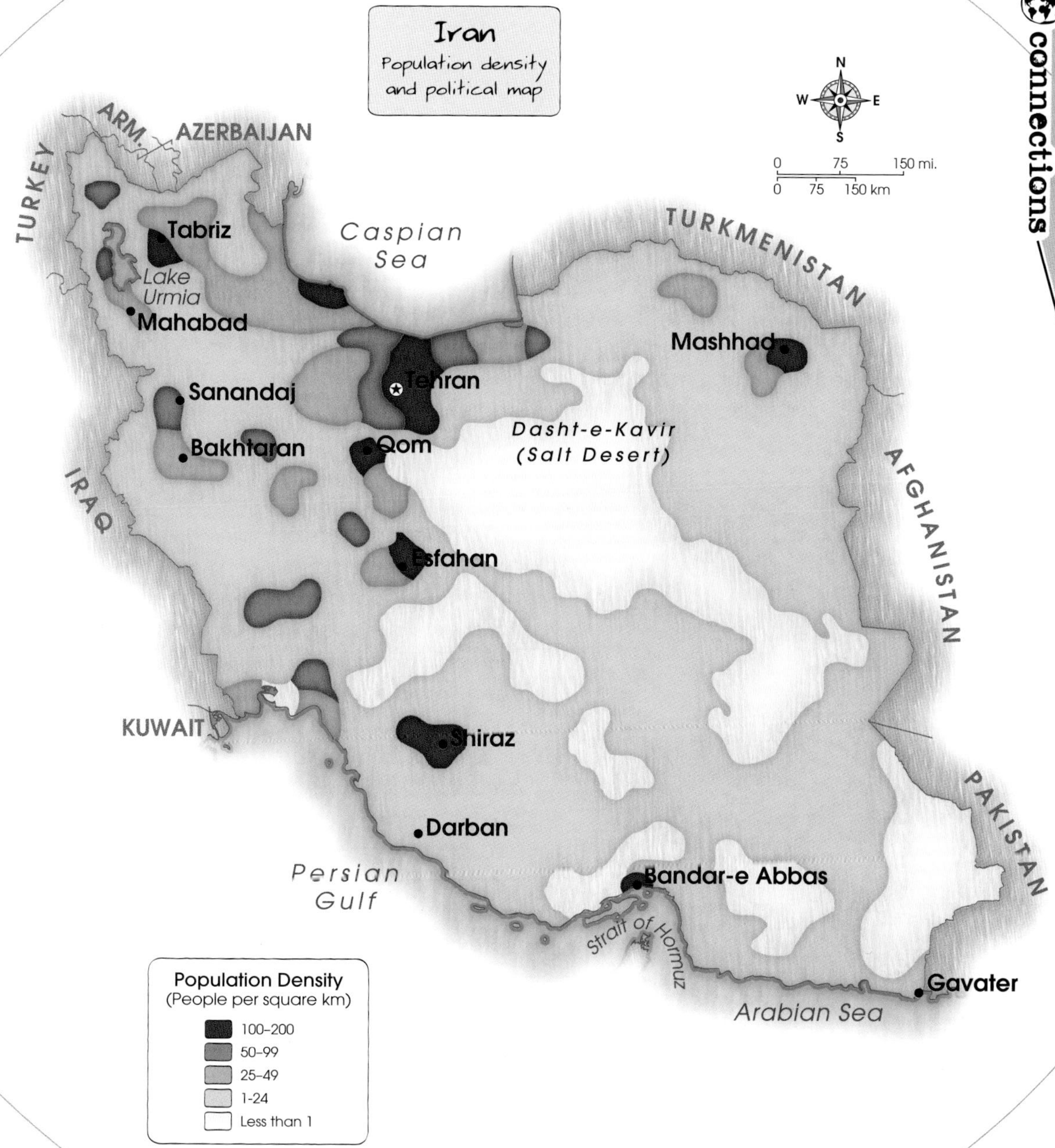

Iran
Population density and political map

N
W — E
S

0   75   150 mi.
0   75   150 km

TURKEY

ARM

AZERBAIJAN

Tabriz

Lake Urmia

Mahabad

Caspian Sea

TURKMENISTAN

Mashhad

Sanandaj

⊛ Tehran

Dasht-e-Kavir (Salt Desert)

IRAQ

Bakhtaran

Qom

AFGHANISTAN

Esfahan

KUWAIT

Shiraz

PAKISTAN

Darban

Persian Gulf

Bandar-e Abbas

Strait of Hormuz

Gavater

Arabian Sea

Population Density
(People per square km)

- 100–200
- 50–99
- 25–49
- 1–24
- Less than 1

Khamenei's View

Supreme Leader Sayyid Ali Khamenei sets many of Iran's policies in the schools and other branches of the government. On April 19, 2005, he spoke to a group of young Iranians who had won medals at an international conference of inventors:

Supreme Leader Sayyid Ali Khamenei (1939–)

The Iranian nation should attain such a high level of scientific progress and development that scholars and scientists in some other parts of the world will find it necessary to learn the Persian language. ... I insist that relevant state organs [government offices] and the media publicize the scientific and technological accomplishments of our talented and brilliant youth. ...

The present achievements of Iranian youngsters in various scientific fields are just the initial steps ... to greater accomplishments, and greater strides should be taken in this direction. Our youngsters should always bear in mind that their present accomplishments indicate that they are capable of reaching the peaks of scientific and technological progress. ...

I hope you will shine in the world with more scientific achievements and technological accomplishments and, thus, bring further honor and glory to our nation.

countries of Turkey, Iraq, Kuwait, and Persian Gulf are on the south and west.

Iranian schools are not all about patriotism and Islam. Iran is strong in teaching science, particularly technology. To help young Iranians become computer literate, for instance, the government is bringing computers into classrooms.

Specialty Schools

Iran's government requires students to attend school through eighth grade, but it does not demand that they go further. After eighth grade, some teenagers from poor families quit school to look for jobs. Good jobs are hard to find for anyone without much education. As a result, most Iranian parents insist that their teenagers attend high school and stay there until graduation. According to the United Nations Children's Fund (UNICEF), about four-fifths of

all Iranian boys and three-quarters of all girls go to high school.

Getting in is not automatic, though. As Iranian teenagers reach the end of eighth grade, they take exams to determine if they've learned enough to attend high school. Students who don't pass the exams have to repeat the eighth grade.

The exams not only decide which students can go on to high school, they also determine which high school they can attend. Up through eighth grade, all Iranian students study the same subjects: reading, arithmetic, history, science, and religion. After eighth grade, students are sent to high schools according to their skills.

Some Iranian high schools teach "general academics." Courses include a variety of subjects such as literature, life sciences (biology, botany, and similar fields), other sciences (generally physics, math,

School Structure in Iran

Type of School	Students' age	Students' grade
Elementary school	6–10 or 11	1st–5th
Middle school (Also called guidance school)	11–13	6th–8th
High school	14–17	9th–12th

and related fields), the arts, and social sciences (history, civics, and economics). These schools are sometimes called theoretical schools because they teach ideas and theories.

Other schools concentrate on particular specialties. Some of them train young Iranians to become clerics. Dozens of other schools dedicate themselves to sciences such as biology, physics, chemistry, and mathematics. Some of these schools rank among the best in the world.

In June 2006, for instance, five of the 33 top prizes at the RoboCup international robot-building competition went to Iranian machines. All of the awards, Iranian and otherwise, went to robots built by college students—except for the robot created by Tehran's Farzanegan High School, which won an award. The next month, at the 2006 International Math Olympiad for high school math students, 498 teenagers on 90 teams from around the world came to test their skills. The six-member Iranian team took eighth place, outdoing teams from nations with strong education systems such as Canada, France, Israel, and England.

While general-academics schools and specialized schools prepare their

In the RoboCup competion, students build robots that compete in soccer matches.

Parents tend to be very protective of their teen daughters, especially in rural areas. If possible, a parent may walk the girl to and from school.

students for college, other schools build skills to use in the workforce right away. These schools train students to become electricians, farmers, metalworkers, tailors, bookkeepers, and other skilled technicians and tradespeople.

City & Country

Schools in big cities such as Tehran tend to do a slightly better job of educating their students than schools out in the country. Urban schools have more money than rural schools, and their equipment tends to be newer and more technologically advanced. Most of Iran's specialized high schools are in urban areas.

On the other hand, says Iranian teacher and writer Malihe Maghazei, "in urban areas, [classes] are very crowded, sometimes with 45 to 50 students." Country classes tend to be smaller, partly because they're not always easy to attend. A city teenager may live only a mile or two from his school, but a rural student may have to travel much farther to get to class.

Attendance can be especially thin in country schools for girls. Many rural families follow old traditions that include keeping their daughters at home to help their parents. In addition, many communities have no schools for girls. For many rural girls, the nearest school is too far away to attend. Parents are hesitant to send their teen daughters on a bus by themselves, even to get to school. Among all Iranian teenagers, rural or urban, rural girls are most likely to drop out of school.

Going Private

Iran's public schools are open to all students, free of charge. For some teenagers and their parents, though, the local middle school or high school may not be good enough. Some public schools provide a poor education because teachers are overworked and underpaid. The most talented teachers know they can be employed in better-paying schools. They do not apply to these public schools. Parents who have enough money sometimes send their children to private school.

Even though the government does not run the private schools, the schools must still obey the government's rules about what to teach and how to teach it. Some teenagers go to private school full time. Others go in addition to public school. They take classes in the late afternoon for advanced instruction that the public school does not provide. Some students go to private school for years. Others take classes for a short period and for a specific reason, such as preparing for a public school's final exams.

Conquering the Exams

A typical Iranian teenager devotes most of his or her evening to homework. More than two hours a night may be spent writing reports, doing math problems,

or working on other assignments.

In addition, Iranian teenagers face the pressure of final exams. Consider this posting from the Internet's Yahoo! Health message board on August 12, 2006:

Hi. I am Mahsa. I am 15 and I am a student of high school in Iran. When I was passing my final exams I was going through a lot of stress. Stress in my body began that

Brain Drain

Iran has the world's highest rate of "brain drain"—that is, intelligent people who move to other countries. According to the International Monetary Fund, which tracks business and education, more than 150,000 college-educated Iranians leave Iran every year. Most of them want to find jobs or pursue higher education.

Most Iranians love their country and do not enjoy leaving it behind. Still, it isn't hard to find Iranians as young as 16 who are thinking about living in a foreign country, if only for a few years.

time that I failed in one of my exams one year ago. Now I can't read composition or a text when there are many people [nearby].

Final exams are important to teens around the world, but they're especially hard on Iranians. A student who does well on the exams can advance from grade to grade and attend college. A student who does poorly may have to repeat a year of school or even drop out.

The most crucial exam is the Konkoor (conquer), the national college entrance exam. This lengthy test asks hundreds of questions. Iranian teens spend months preparing for it as intensely as soldiers train for combat. Their future rests on how well they do. If their work on the test fails to qualify them for college, they will have a hard time finding a decent job. Most employers want to hire college graduates.

Many colleges, including Tehran University, are coeducational, teaching men and women together.

Iranian law requires women to wear long coats or robes and cover their heads with hejabs. In urban areas, teen girls tend to modernize their dress with colorful scarves and tailored overcoats.

2

Living the Day to Day

WHAT IS DAILY LIFE LIKE IN IRAN? That is a hard question. A rich and rebellious girl in Tehran does not live like a young man in the holy city of Qom who is studying to become a Muslim cleric. Visitors from Tabriz might seem almost like foreigners to people from Gavater. After all, Gavater is a seacoast village on the Gulf of Oman, while Tabriz—1,500 miles (2,600 km) to the northwest—is a mountain city of 1.5 million.

Still, most Iranian teenagers do share a few things in common. Waves of religion wash through their lives. Whether or not they are Muslims, Islam is an important factor in daily life.

But that is not all that life is about. Currents of secrecy, patriotism, and hospitality flow around Iranians. Money, clothes, food, government restrictions, and ordinary household concerns often rise up to command their attention. And like kids everywhere, Iran's teenagers are always looking for things to enjoy.

Iran & Islam

These quotations from Iran's constitution show the importance of Islam in Iranian life.

- All civil, penal, financial, economic, administrative, cultural, military, political, and other laws and regulations must be based on Islamic criteria [rules].
- Public gatherings and marches may be freely held, provided ... that they are not detrimental [harmful] to the fundamental principles of Islam.
- Courts of justice ... are to be formed in accordance with the criteria of Islam.
- Everyone has the right to choose any occupation he wishes, if it is not contrary to Islam.
- The Army of the Islamic Republic of Iran must be an Islamic Army—i.e. [that is], committed to Islamic ideology [ideas].
- Publications and the press have freedom of expression except when it is detrimental to the fundamental principles of Islam.

Keeping the Faith

"In the name of Allah, the Compassionate, the Merciful ... " That line, or something similar, launches government documents and speeches throughout Iran. In the nation with the official title Islamic Republic of Iran, Islam is everywhere. Most of the people are Muslims, and the government enforces the faith's teachings.

In particular, the government enforces Twelve-Imam Shia Islam, a specific form of Islam. Muslims believe that Muhammad (570–632) was Allah's (God's) last and greatest prophet. In 656, Muslims broke into two groups, Sunnis and Shiites, because of differences in beliefs. Most Muslims in the world are Sunnis who believe that the first four Muslim leaders after the prophet Muhammad were proper guides for the faithful. In Iran, most Muslims are Shiites, who believe that Muhammad's only true heir was his cousin and son-in-law Ali. They call Ali the first imam, a virtually perfect religious leader.

After Ali came 11 other imams, all of them decedents of Ali's line of family members. Shiites believe that the last one, the 10th-century Imam Mahdi, never died. They expect him to re-emerge as a messiah. In the meantime, high-ranking religious leaders called ayatollahs have guided the faithful, particularly in Iran.

The most important ayatollah is the supreme leader. This man has the final word on all matters of Iranian politics

The 290-member Majlis meets in the parliament building in the capital city, Tehran. The grand building can hold 800 spectators.

and religion. He is more powerful than all other Iranian officials, including the president.

Iran's government works by a series of elections. An 86-member Assembly of Experts elects the supreme leader for life and advises him on important decisions. A group of officials called the Guardian Council selects the candidates for the assembly, and the Iranian people hold an election to pick the winners. The 12-member council also can approve or turn down laws that come out of

Iran's lawmaking body, the Majlis-e-Shura-ye-Eslami (Islamic Consultative Assembly). The assembly is referred to as the Majlis for short.

The council has two types of members. Six of them are clerics selected by the supreme leader. The other six are experts in Iranian law. Iran's most important judges choose them. The Majlis can accept or reject the judges' choices.

The system may sound complicated, but the result is that Iran's government enforces strict Sharia, the

Under Sharia, the faces of women cannot be used in advertising and product packaging. Market owners cover the faces on imported products.

Islamic law. Sharia covers every aspect of life: eating, drinking, talking, behavior toward parents, conduct in business, the proper length of a man's beard, and hundreds of other topics.

Sharia can be hard to obey, but many Iranians say they like it. In May and June 2006, the polling firm Zogby International asked 810 Iranians, "Would you most like to see Iran's society become more secular and liberal, more religious and conservative, or just stay as it is?" The most popular response—from 36 percent of everyone questioned—was "more conservative and religious."

Nevertheless, many young Iranians

don't want politicians and policemen telling them how to live. Many of them distrust and resent the clerics who control the government. Others revere Allah and the prophet Muhammad but also love non-Muslim influences such as American music and European fashions.

Quite a few Iranians live two lives. They are strictly obedient and proper in public but relaxed and even self-indulgent behind closed doors. "When we were six, we already knew there were two worlds: one at home and one at school," one young Iranian admitted to the blog View From Iran. "We knew how to keep secrets. Soon, we understood who we could joke with and who we had to tell that our parents prayed 100 times a day." As a result, View From Iran says, the government has produced "millions of brilliant liars."

They feel the need to lie because the police are often watching. The Iranian government disapproves of people who oppose the government's rules or simply follow their own desires. Article 609 of Iran's Penal Code (the list of punishments for crimes) lays the rules out clearly.

Anyone who insults a government leader "should be punished by imprisonment from three to six months or whipping (74 lashes) or a fine of 50,000 to 1,000,000 rial" (U.S.$5.41 to $108).

Iranian police have arrested or beaten teenagers and others who publicly hold hands, take photographs, or play music. Most teens, even those who have never suffered police punishment, know about it and work hard to keep from experiencing it.

A policewoman (back to camera) watched as a young man and woman greeted each other with a kiss. The couple was soon restrained for breaking Sharia.

The Different Ones

The Iranian government does not insist that everyone believe in Islam. The government makes an exception for Jews, Christians, and Zoroastrians. Iran's constitution allows members of these religions to worship, live, and raise children by the rules of their faith. Nevertheless, members of those faiths have to obey Islamic laws and cannot hold powerful government jobs.

In addition, the government has virtually outlawed another faith, Baha'i. The Baha'i faith is one of the newest world religions, and it was born in Iran. In 1844, Siyyid 'Ali-Muhammad, a mystic from the Persian city of Shiraz, began preaching that a messiah was coming. His followers called him the

Bab (gate) to a new faith and called themselves Babis. The Bab's teachings offended and alarmed the Islamic authorities so much that in 1850,

Religion in Iran

Shia Islam
89%

Other
(includes Zoroastrianism, Judaism, Christianity, and Baha'i)
2%

Sunni Islam
9%

Source: United States Central Intelligence Agency. *The World Factbook—Iran.*

A young Iranian Jew performs a morning prayer ritual. Tehran's 17,000 Jews have their own kosher restaurants, schools, and places of worship.

Followers of Zarotoshtra

Zoroastrians are followers of a prophet who was based in Iran. In Persian, he is known as Zaratoshtra or Zartosht. In Western cultures, he is known as Zoraster, the name the Greeks gave him. Experts say that he was born in 628 B.C. or 660 B.C. or 1000 B.C.—or maybe 6184 B.C. And his birthplace is just as uncertain.

In a world where many religions had several gods, Zaratoshtra was one of the first to preach that there was only one God. This God, named Ahura-Mazda, wanted people to practice good thoughts, good words, and good deeds. The faith's symbol is a flame, and its most important principle is asha, which means truth, righteousness, and order.

Zoroastrianism was the religion of most Iranians until Islam swept through the country in the 600s. These days, the world has fewer than 200,000 Zoroastrians, primarily in Iran and India.

Zoroastrian girls dress in traditional clothing for a festival.

they had him killed. In a fury, some of the Babis tried to kill Nasser al-Din, the shah, or ruler, of then Persia. The shah killed thousands of Babis and imprisoned others.

In 1852, a Babi prisoner named Mirza Husayn-Ali had a vision revealing that he was the messiah the Bab had predicted. In 1863, after he had been released from prison, he took the name Baha'u'llah, which means "glory of God." He traveled through the Middle East and western Asia and wrote books that became sacred writings of the Baha'i faith.

Baha'is believe there is one God and that all religions are more or less different versions of the same thing. In addition, Baha'is

take the coming of Baha'u'llah as a sign that humanity is starting to become truly mature, peaceful, and just.

The government's opposition to the Baha'i faith is clear. Authorities refuse to let Baha'is attend college. Baha'is can lose their jobs for attending their own worship services. And the government punishes Baha'is for little or no reason. On May 19, 2006, for instance, authorities in the city of Shiraz arrested 54 Baha'is, some as young as 15, for teaching in a non-Islamic school.

Iran's Ethnicities

In addition to people of different faiths, Iran includes people from different cultural backgrounds.

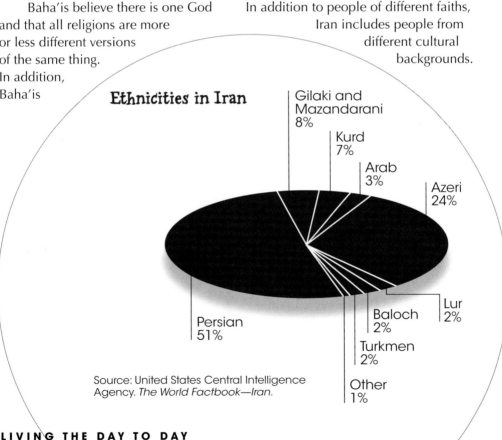

Ethnicities in Iran

- Gilaki and Mazandarani 8%
- Kurd 7%
- Arab 3%
- Azeri 24%
- Lur 2%
- Baloch 2%
- Turkmen 2%
- Other 1%
- Persian 51%

Source: United States Central Intelligence Agency. *The World Factbook—Iran.*

Persians descend from an empire that grew out of south-central Iran's province of Fars. Their group, which includes President Mahmoud Ahmadinejad, adds up to a little over half of all Iranians but fills most of the top posts in the national government. Some members of other groups resent the Persians. They view Persians as snobs who see themselves as more civilized than other Iranians.

Among the non-Persian Iranians, about half—including Supreme Leader Khameini—are Azeri. Their territory lies in northwest Iran near the border with Azerbaijan, the nation that used to control the area. In general, Azeris have risen higher in government and business than other Iranian minorities. At the same time, they sometimes protest what they see as Persian insensitivity to their rights and dignity.

Southwest of the Azeris are the Kurds, who number about 7 percent of the population. Their traditional land overlaps parts of Iran, Iraq, and Turkey. Arabs, about 3 percent of all Iranians, mostly live further south, in or near the province of Khuzestan. Like the people of nearby Saudi Arabia, Iran's Arabs usually speak Arabic as their main language. Iran also has Turks, Baluchis, Lurs, Turkmens, and members of other groups.

In the 1970s, large numbers of rural Kurds moved to Kurdish cities, including Bakhtaran, Sanandaj, and Mahabad.

None of Iran's ethnic groups have declared independence or organized any all-out uprisings. Most Iranians are strongly patriotic, with a fierce pride in their country's beauty and independence. Even Iranians who dislike their government speak out against any interference from other countries.

The Trouble with Women

"The good women are ... obedient," according to Chapter 4, Verse 34, of the Qur'an. It is one of the book's most famous passages. Other verses call men and women equal, but Iranian law puts men first.

In some ways, Iran is one of the most just and fair places for women in its part of the world. Iranian women own businesses, serve in the Majlis, and fill all sorts of other roles.

Men still dominate the country, though. For instance, women hold only 4.1 percent of the Majlis' seats. Nearly every Iranian applauds the country's championship soccer teams, but only

Female members of the Majlis are seated in front of the male members during lawmaking sessions.

In cities, it is common to see a wide range of clothing, from Western fashions to conservative chadors.

males may attend the games because Sharia forbids women and girls to look at bare-legged men. Iran's Penal Code says that a murderer must pay his victim's family for what he has done, but the fine for murdering a woman is half the amount for murdering a man. In some court cases, it takes the testimony of two women to equal the word of one man. These laws affect teenagers as well as adults, since many areas of Iranian law consider girls as young as 9 to be grown women.

In addition, males and females must enter public places such as airports, government offices, and university buildings through separate doorways. On buses and other public transportation, they sit in separate sections.

The Qur'an has a special instruction for women: "Do not display your finery," which could grab male

A Dangerous Escape

Iran's Drug Control Headquarters admits that at least 13 percent of the country's teenagers and college students—well over a million people—are in danger of becoming drug addicts. Possibly the most popular drug is one of the deadliest: opium.

Iran has the world's highest rate of opium abuse. The United Nations Office on Drugs and Crime's 2006 World Drug Report says that 2.8 percent of all Iranians from ages 15 to 64 use opium. That's much higher than the rate of neighboring nations such as Pakistan (0.8 percent), Turkmenistan (0.3 percent), Saudi Arabia (0.01 percent), or Turkey (0.05 percent). Among Iranian high school students, the rate is up to 3.5 percent.

Opium can provide a warm sense of serenity. Young Iranians use it to escape their troubles, but it is highly addictive. An overdose can kill.

The problem will probably not go away soon because opium is easy to get. One of the world's largest opium-producing nations is Afghanistan, on Iran's eastern border.

attention. From rules like these come hejab, the Islamic dress code that literally covers all females from age 9 on up. (The word *hejab* also means a scarf that covers a woman's hair.) They must hide every inch of their skin except faces and hands.

Traditional women wear the *chador,* a word that literally means "tent." This large, semicircular, long veil is placed on the head. It covers the entire body except for the face. More stylish women and girls wear the *manteau* (a long overcoat) but tailor it to show off their curves. They cover their heads with a scarf or head veil but adjust it to let a little hair fly free.

chador
cha-DOOR

manteau
maan-TOO

Inside their homes, some women and girls ignore the rules—but not outside. Breaking the law carries strict punishment. Violators can be imprisoned from 10 days to two months or pay a fine of 50,000 to 500,000 rial (U.S.$5 to $54). Some women and girls enjoy the rules of hejab. Covering up is a part of their faith, and it protects them from unwelcome stares.

Many others, especially teenagers and other young women, dislike the rules. They find keeping themselves covered at all times is a nuisance. What's more, they resent that men and boys don't have to hide themselves. A blogger who calls herself Iranian Girl wrote:

I go to work every day, [and] while my male colleagues wear cool T-shirts, I have to stand [in] my heavy, warm, dark, long clothes. ... I can remember the last time I could feel the wind blowing around my neck and moving my hair, what a great pleasure, I was about eight years old.

Since they cannot show much skin, many young Iranian women draw attention to the bits that they can show.

Many wear heavy, elaborate makeup to emphasize their faces, particularly their eyes. In fashionable parts of Tehran and other cities, teenagers from well-off families pay doctors to change their faces. Cosmetic surgery is so popular that high school and college girls proudly wear the small, white bandage that indicates a recent nose job. Tehran has acquired the nickname "the nose job capital of the world."

Though legal cosmetics are available in stores, 85 percent of beauty products used in Iran are smuggled into the country illegally. These products, mainly from China, India, Pakistan, and Turkey, are less expensive than the legal ones.

City Life

More than two-thirds of Iran's people live in its cities. According to the United Nations Population Division, Iran is in the top one-third of the most urbanized nations in the world.

Like cities in other countries, Iranian cities are a combination of old and new. The newer areas usually house the wealthiest citizens, the offices where they work, the stores and restaurants that serve them, and the schools that teach their children. The older neighborhoods tend to have more mosques and the busy marketplaces called bazaars.

Iran's biggest city is the capital, Tehran. Its 254 square miles (658 sq km) make it about the same size as Athens, Greece, or Baghdad, Iraq, and it is larger than Philadelphia, Pennsylvania. More than 8 million people live in Tehran. Another 6 million or more fill the surrounding suburbs.

Much of Tehran looks nothing like a place suffering under a harsh government. Leafy trees line clean streets. The city's wealthy northern side slopes up toward the beautiful Elburz mountain range. Teens happily play soccer in the city's 800-some parks.

Though the parks are peaceful, the roadways are not. Many Tehranis and other urban Iranians drive like rocket-propelled madmen, when they can move

Many of Tehran's parks feature paths for walking, biking, and roller blading.

Without new road developments and stronger traffic laws, Tehran's traffic problems are expected to become even worse. Experts estimate that the number of vehicles on the road will double to about 30 million over the next 10 years.

at all. Traffic jams clog the streets. Any driver who can whip past another will do it, whether the move is safe or not.

The traffic produces some of the world's worst smog. The World Bank, an organization that tracks working conditions, ranks Tehran among the world's five cities most polluted by the poisonous gas sulfur dioxide. The cars also fill the air with millions of tiny but solid and often poisonous objects called particulates.

For all of its problems, Tehran is one of the most exciting places in the country, where the nation's political, financial, and cultural leaders decide how the citizens will live. It is also the place where teenagers are most likely to break or bend the rules.

Iran's other cities are nothing to ignore, either. "Esfahan *nesf-e jahan*" is an old saying that means "Esfahan [is] half the world." The city's huge factories make steel, refine oil, and build airplane parts, and its nuclear reactors attract international spies. But it is also one of Iran's most beautiful places. This oasis in Iran's desert, 273 miles (439 km) south of Tehran, attracts masses of tourists who visit its gorgeous ancient mosques, elaborate bridges, and busy bazaars.

Esfahan's 1.6 million people make it Iran's third most populous city. Mashad, in northeastern Iran near the Turkmenistan border, is even bigger. Mashad is home to about 2.5 million people, but it rarely makes huge national news. It is a conservative religious city, where religious pilgrims come to visit historical sites.

Esfahan is home to one of the world's most beautiful plazas, Meidun-e-Emam.

In mountain villages, mud homes are built into the slopes above a flat valley.

Country Folks

Iran has other large cities, including exotic Tabriz, sophisticated Shiraz, and devout Qom. Still, most of Iran is rural.

Visitors to rural Iran sometimes feel like they have stepped back in time. The air is perfectly clean, people live in homes made of brick and mud, and shepherds lead flocks to grazing land. At the same time, virtually all of Iran is hooked up to electricity, and many homes have modern appliances.

Rural Iranians are among the nation's most conservative people, but—in a nation famous for its hospitality—they are also among the most

Many homes have little furniture, and family members prefer to relax on their plush rugs and cushions.

eager to welcome visitors. After all, they have few other diversions. As Malihe Maghazei wrote in 2005, "In many small cities and villages, there are no playgrounds, stadiums, theaters, public libraries, or even parks." As a result, young country people have been moving away to the big cities.

Be It Ever So Humble

Homes in the country are small, often not much more than a room or two. Naturally, teenagers in those homes don't usually have their own bedrooms.

Instead of preparing a bed for a guest, for instance, a rural family might lay cushions and blankets out on the floor. There might not even be a mattress.

In the country or the city, an Iranian home is likely to have thick and often ornately knotted Persian rugs. Some of them are as plush and comfortable as any bed.

In major urban areas, most people live in apartments. Housing is expensive. The blogger Iranian Girl complains, "I should save it [my entire salary] for 13 years to be able to buy the smallest cheapes[t] apartment in the worst location in Tehran, I should pay all my monthly salary to rent that apartment!" People in suburbs and smaller cities live in apartments or small houses.

The only Iranian teenagers who have rooms of their own are members of upper-income families who live in mansions or luxury apartments. These teens are likely to decorate the walls of their bedrooms with posters of football (soccer) stars.

Eating & Drinking

As any parent can tell you, teenagers love food. In Iran, as in most countries, the day starts with breakfast. Iranian breakfasts are usually fairly simple: bread with jam; a salty, white cheese called feta; and *chai*, a dark, spicy tea.

Eggs are fairly common in Iranian breakfasts, as is a porridge called *halim*.

Lunch is often the day's biggest meal. It almost always features at least one meat dish—usually chicken, lamb, or beef—as well as rice, bread, salad, a vegetable dish, and plain yogurt.

chai
cha-EEI

halim
ha-LEEM

A Day in the Life of an Iranian Teen

Teens, like most Iranians, wake up early—no later than an hour or two after sunrise. Families eat breakfast together, then head off to work or school. Children who attend school are in class until early- to mid-afternoon. After-school activities include watching television, hanging out with friends, playing sports, or getting private tutoring. Girls may be expected to help their mothers with housework. Rural teens may help out on the farm.

Following dinner with the family, teens complete their homework and head to bed. In addition, Shiites are supposed to pray three times a day, although not all of them do.

Some days have a different routine. Since the Muslim Sabbath is Friday, the weekend begins on Thursday evening. Many businesses shut down even earlier. On Friday evenings, everyone is supposed to attend prayers at a mosque. Many Iranians, especially Tehranis, skip the prayers. They simply use Friday for fun and relaxation with family and friends.

Afterward, in the late afternoon, many Iranians take a break for chai.

Dinner usually starts around 8 or 9 P.M. One course is almost always a kebab—chunks of chicken, lamb, or beef grilled on a skewer. Pork is never served. Islam forbids Muslims to eat it. Dinners also include salad, yogurt, tea, bread, and rice.

For dinner or other meals, many Iranians love to picnic. On most weekends when weather permits, Iranian families and friends happily head outdoors with food and blankets.

On picnics and in almost every other meal, Iranians enjoy rice. Many dishes are served on a bed of rice. *Polow*—steamed and spiced rice pilaf—is an Iranian specialty.

Stew is popular, too. *Khoresht-e fesenjan*, for example, mixes chicken, walnuts, pomegranate juice, and sugar. *Abgusht* is a thick lamb stew,

polow
po-LO

khoresht-e fesenjan
kor-esht-EH fes-en-JAAN

Picnics are so popular among Iranians that even snow won't keep them inside.

Though the U.S. government bans U.S. companies from doing business in Iran, exceptions are made for food and beverage products, including Coca-Cola.

and *ghorme sabzi* combines meat and green vegetables.

Soup is another Iranian favorite, especially yogurt soups and the noodle soup *aash-e reshteh*. Bread is a part of most meals, too, and vegetables such as spinach show up in quite a few dishes. On hot days, watermelons are popular. Always popular is the strong, earthy spice saffron. Iranians use it as much as people in other cultures use salt. Nuts and fruits, particularly citrus fruits such as oranges, are favorite side dishes and snacks. In the big cities, teenagers love fast food such as pizza.

No teenager likes to skip dessert.

abgusht
aab-GOOSHT

ghorme sabzi
kor-MEH sab-ZEE

aash-e reshteh
aash-eh resh-TEH

Sholeh-zard is a sweet rice pudding. Halvah is a fudgy treat made from grains such as wheat or sesame seed, plus saffron, rose water, sugar, and butter. And teens in Iran love cookies, cakes, and ice cream as much as teens anywhere.

With food comes drink. Virtually everyone drinks tea, but many Iranians like fruit drinks and even America's popular drink, Coca-Cola. Alcohol is against Islamic law for everyone, both adults and teenagers. A boy or girl caught with a beer can face arrest, heavy fines, and lashes with a whip. Still, a small minority of teenagers do drink, since many Iranian parents smuggle alcohol into the home. Upon request, sellers who keep stashes of the forbidden product in their homes will deliver right to the customer's home.

sholeh-zard
show-leh-ZARD

Yasha is so proud of his family that he risks arrest by having their initials tatooed on his back.

3

The Nearest & Dearest

"TATTOOS HAVE BECOME A FAD AMONG MANY YOUNG IRANIAN[S], who proudly display them in private but must keep them under wraps," Associated Press journalist Brian Murphy reported in 2006. The government forbids tattoos. People who wear them risk arrest. One such outlaw, Murphy wrote, is a college student named Yasha. What did this young rebel hire his tattoo artist to draw? "Yasha now sports the English letters KMKKY to represent the names of his family members." Family is so important to Iranians that a young lawbreaker would risk jail to honor his relatives. Most Iranians have barely enough money to survive, and nearly everyone is afraid of the police. It's only natural that they turn to their relatives for comfort, love, and joy. Iranian-American Sara Nobari observed family life as she visited Iranian relatives in 2005. "The spontaneity [eagerness] Iranians show when offered a chance to get together with family surpassed any I thought I possessed." When she gave them some privacy, "they were confused; why sit apart when you can join family?"

The average Iranian mother has one or two children. By contrast, the world's average is 2.59. Mothers in Iraq average 4.18, and Afghan mothers average 6.69.

An Iranian family is more than parents and offspring. Aunts, uncles, cousins, grandparents, and others are a part of daily life. They visit often. Sometimes they stay for an afternoon or evening, and sometimes for days or longer. Even dead relatives remain a part of Iranian life. Iran's war with Iraq, which ran from 1980 through 1988, killed or crippled a generation of young men. Families warmly remember them, and government announcements still praise the war's victims as martyrs.

Playing the Roles

"Between a man and a woman," says Article 1105 of the Iranian laws called the Civil Code, "the position of the head of the family is the exclusive right of the husband." In conservative communities, fathers tend to control their teenagers. In modernized areas such as northern Tehran, fathers take a lighter approach.

Almost everywhere, fathers are fiercely loyal to their kids. And mothers are as loyal as fathers. If a teacher punishes a teenage boy or girl too harshly, the teen's parents may head to the school and angrily criticize the teacher.

Many Iranian mothers have jobs outside the home. But society expects them to be expert housekeepers as

well. "Nearly every ... Persian mother I've met runs her home like a five star hotel," says Tess Strand Alipour, an American who moved to Iran.

Iranian parents adore and sometimes even indulge their children.

The majority of daily child care is the mother's responsibility.

However, they want the kids to work, too. Mothers and fathers expect their teenagers to do well in school and help out around the house (especially the daughters). In addition, parents worry about whether their children (especially the sons) will be able to make a decent living, since jobs are hard to find in Iran.

Friendship, Iranian Style

Teenagers who live under Iran's religious government and high-pressure education system need friends. As a result, Iranian teenagers keep in close contact. After school, for instance, they meet to play sports or go shopping. The ones who can afford cell phones eagerly trade text messages and ringtones.

In Iran, one out of every 16 people has a cell phone. That's a lower rate than Middle Eastern neighbors such as Saudi Arabia (with one phone for every three people). At the same time, it's a higher rate than Asian neighbors such as Pakistan (one phone for every 33 people) or Afghanistan (one phone for every 97 people).

Even more important than cell phones is the Internet. One-tenth to one-third of all young Iranians have Internet access. It is most available in Tehran and other big cities. Not everyone can afford an Internet connection, but major cities have plenty of Internet cafes where teens can log on for a while. And young Iranians aren't just logging on; they're writing. The number of Persian language blogs ranges from 60,000 to 100,000. Experts estimate that among these online journals, Persian is the Internet's third or fourth most common language.

Bloggers have to be careful, though. The government blocks access

Twenty-five-year-old Parastoo Dokouhaki runs one of Iran's most popular blogs, using her real name. She says she is careful to stay within the government's guidelines.

to sites posting messages that it considers disloyal, anti-Islamic, or otherwise un-Iranian. If the site originates from inside Iran, the government tries to shut it down. If possible, the people who created it will be punished. To protect themselves, some bloggers post their messages in foreign languages.

Despite the dangers, young Iranians keep logging on. The Internet is one of the places where they feel most free to communicate.

Boys & Girls

Marriage is an important part of both Islam and Iranian life. The Qur'an's Chapter 30, Verse 21, spells it out: "He [Allah] created mates for you from yourselves that you may find rest in them." To make it easy for people to find that restful place, the government has set

Who's Who

If you live in Iran and your name is Muhammad or Fatemah, you are not alone. Here are some common Iranian names and their meanings.

Boys

Name	Meaning
Ali	Muhammad's successor
Hamid	Worthy of praise
Hussein	Good
Mehdi	Guided
Muhammad	the name of Islam's founder

Girls

Name	Meaning
Fatemah	Muhammad's daughter
Maryam	Mary, mother of Jesus
Shirin	Sweet
Yasmin	Jasmine (a flower)
Zahra	White or shining

49

up the Imam Reza Love Fund. The fund is named after one of Shia Islam's 12 imams. It offers newlyweds low-cost loans.

Many young men and their mothers are constantly hunting for brides. "Being single is not that easy over here with a culture where marriage is a sacred duty," says a young blogger calling herself Proshat. "With every wedding I attend to, a lot of people try to bribe me into getting a hold of a good chap and settling down!"

In conservative areas, parents arrange their teenagers' marriages and even their dates. When parents spot a possible mate for their teenager, they call the potential spouse's parents. The four parents meet to discuss matters such as the boy's career plans and family background. (Under traditional Iranian customs, the parents pay somewhat less attention to the girl.) If both sets of parents approve, they bring the boy and girl together. Everyone wants the two to fall for each other, but love is not completely necessary.

In modernized places such as Tehran, teenagers often seek partners themselves. Some of them look for prospects at shopping malls and fast-food restaurants. A young Tehrani with a car might drive slowly up a popular street. He'll hand a card with name and contact information to nearly anyone who looks attractive and available.

They have to be careful, though. Sharia forbids women and girls to meet with males who are not their relatives. The police are always watching for anyone getting too friendly with the opposite sex. To meet people safely, some teenagers secretly arrange house parties. When the weather allows,

Teen boys are obvious with their attention as they look for girls in front of a mall.

Although the mountains near Darban provide a secluded place for boys and girls to be together, the girls keep their hejab on just in case the authorities come around.

young Iranians go hiking or skiing in the mountains, where there aren't many police.

Whether teenagers meet on their own or through their parents' arrangements, dating in Iran is dangerous. Simple flirting can alert the police. Hugging and kissing can bring heavy fines, painful beatings, or prison sentences. Sexual activity can bring on lashes with a whip, and being gay can invite the death penalty.

To get around these rules, many young Iranians try temporary marriages. These arrangements are permitted under Shia Islam. A temporary marriage can last for weeks or for hours. It frees Iranians to kiss in public and enjoy other forms of contact. When a temporary marriage ends, the couple usually splits apart without the emotional agony of a divorce. As they separate, the "husband" generally gives the "bride" some money.

51

Young women light candles to mark the last day of Ashura, a 10-day mourning period that marks the anniversary of Hussein's martyrdom in 680.

4

Holidays, Holy Days, & Other Days

IRANIANS CELEBRATE AND GRIEVE WITH PASSION. Their country has two kinds of holidays, Islamic and non-Islamic. Since Iran is officially an Islamic nation, Islamic holidays are national holidays.

Some of the most important holidays honor the deaths of the prophet Muhammad; his successor, Ali; and Ali's son and successor, Hussein. Hussein's holiday, for instance, remembers the date in 680 when he died fighting a ruler who ordered him to quit Islam. On this holiday, called Ashura, mournful Shiites wear black.

They march in funerallike processions and listen to stories or re-enactments of Hussein's martyrdom.

Happier holidays include Mawlid al-Nabi (Muhammad's birthday) and the birthdays of leaders such as the savior Imam Mahdi. Happy times like these are sometimes called eid (feasts or festivals). Among the biggest eid are Eid al-Fitr (the Feast of Breaking the Fast) and Eid al-Adha (the

eid
eeid

53

Religious Holidays

For religious holidays, Iran uses an ancient Islamic calendar. Its year runs 10 to 12 days shorter than the Gregorian calendar, which most of the world uses. As a result, its holidays shift from season to season.

Religious Holiday	Islamic Calendar	Gregorian Calendar
Eid al-Adha (Feast of the Sacrifice)	Zihajja 10	late December to late January
Ashura (Martyrdom of Hussein)	Moharram 10	late January to late February
Death of Muhammad and martyrdom of Ali	Safar 28	early to late March
Mawlid al-Nabi (Birthday of Muhammad)	Rabi-ol-Avi 17	late March to late April
Unity Week	Rabi-ol-Avi	April 12 to17
Birthday of Imam Mahdi	Sha'ban 15	late August to late September
Eid al-Fltr (Feast of Breaking the Fast)	Shawwal 1	mid-October to late November

Feast of the Sacrifice).

Eid al-Fitr ends the holy month of Ramadan, when Muslims may not eat, drink, or take anything by mouth until sunset. Iranians celebrate the eid with prayers and elaborate meals. Eid al-Adha recalls Chapter 22 in the Biblical book of Genesis, when God called Abraham to sacrifice his son Isaac. At the last moment, God told Abraham to slaughter a ram or lamb instead. To celebrate God's mercy, Muslims sacrifice lambs and eat them. As a result, the price of sheep skyrockets around this time of year.

National Days

Among the nonreligious holidays, the most festive is Norooz (New Day), the Iranian calendar's New Year. Norooz falls on the first day of spring. Its parties, dinners, family gatherings, and vacation trips can continue for nearly two weeks.

The fun starts on the Wednesday before Norooz with the fire festival, Chaharshanbeh Souri (Red Wednesday or

National Holidays

Events in Iranian history appear on the traditional Iranian calendar, which uses different months from the Gregorian calendar.

National Holiday	Iranian Calendar	Gregorian Calendar
Victory of the Islamic Revolution Day	Bahman 22	late December to late January
Chaharshanbeh Souri (Red Wednesday)	Last Wednesday in Esfand	late January to late February
Oil Nationalization Day	Estand 29	March 20
Norooz (Iranian New Year)	Farvardin 1	March 21
Islamic Republic Day	Farvardin 12	April 1
Sizdah-Bedar (Nature Day)	Farvardin 13	April 2
Death of Khomeini	Khordad 14	June 4
Revolt of Khordad 15	Khordad 15	June 5

Fiery Wednesday). The festival comes from Iran's ancient Zoroastrian faith. At fire-festival parties, teenagers and others celebrate the end of winter by jumping over bonfires while shouting or singing, *"Sorkheeyeh toe az man, zardeeyeh man az toe!"* This means "Give me your red glow, and take away my paleness." The paleness comes from being indoors all winter.

On the new year's 13th day is the national nature day, Sizdah-Bedar (Getting Rid of Thirteen or Thirteen Outdoors). Like other people, Iranians

Chaharshanbeh Souri has been celebrated for thousands of years, since the beginning of the Zoroastrianism in Iran.

have considered the number 13 unlucky. Tradition encourages them to get rid of the bad luck by spending the day amid the beauty of nature. It's a chance for teens to indulge in two favorite Iranian customs: picnicking and escaping into the hills.

Other holidays celebrate government milestones. Oil Nationalization Day, for instance, honors an event that took place in 1951. Then-prime minister Muhammad Mosaddeq took Iran's enormously rich oil industry away from the British company that controlled it.

Coming of Age

Iranian teenagers rarely celebrate growing up with an event like a sweet 16 party or bar mitzvah. Iran's government, though, sets definite ages for adulthood.

Iranians can drive and vote at the same age, 18. The nation has no legal drinking age, since Islam forbids alcohol.

For most other purposes, according to Article 49 of the country's Penal Code, adulthood starts at 15 for boys and 9 for girls. At 9, a girl can get married if her father approves. If she commits a crime, she can pay the full penalty, including death.

The Khomeini Holidays

Some major holidays honor Ayatollah Ruhollah Khomeini, the most revered person in modern Iranian history.

Historians are unsure of Khomeini's birthdate. It is believed to be either on May 17, 1900, or September 24, 1902. He was named Ruhollah Musavi at birth. His hometown was the Iranian farm village of Khomein, about 84 miles (135 km) southwest of Qom. (The name Khomeini means "of Khomein.") He came from a religious family that claimed the prophet Muhammad among its ancestors.

Khomeini became an Islamic scholar. He was convinced that Islam could solve the world's problems. Over the years, he turned to politics. By the early 1960s, he was getting fed up with Iran's shah, Reza Pahlavi, who did not support Islamic rule. In January 1963, the shah declared the "white revolution." It was a series of reforms that Khomeini and others believed would make Iran less Islamic and more like Europe or North America. Khomeini began leading a protest movement.

In early June, the shah's forces tried to stop Khomeini by jailing him. Soon afterward, though, on the 15th of the Persian month of Khordad,

Khomeini's followers rose up in protest. Although government troops slaughtered mobs of the protesters, Khordad 15 (June 5) established Khomeini as a hero.

The shah eventually let Khomeini out of jail. Khomeini kept criticizing him, and on November 4, 1964, Iranian

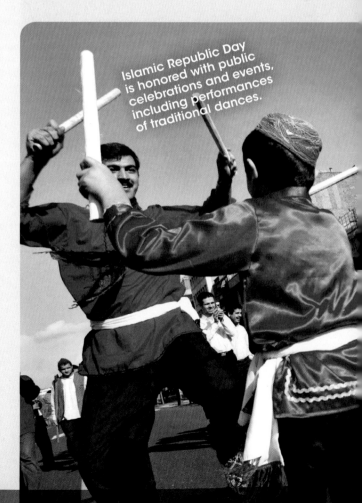

Islamic Republic Day is honored with public celebrations and events, including performances of traditional dances.

authorities arrested Khomeini again and expelled him from Iran. For the next 14 years, he traveled from country to country, encouraging Iranians to fight the shah.

In the late 1970s, a rising number of Iranians demanded that the shah leave Iran. On January 16, 1979, he did. On February 1, Khomeini returned to Iran. His forces seized control of the government 10 days later—a date that Iran celebrates as Victory of the Islamic Revolution Day. On April 1, Khomeini declared Iran an Islamic republic. That date has stood as Islamic Republic Day ever since.

Iran wasn't an easy place for Khomeini to lead. Sunnis and Shiites often argued over the proper way to live an Islamic life and govern an Islamic country. They even argued about the date when Muhammad was born. Sunnis said it was the 12th day of the month Rabi ol-Aval, while Shiites said it was the 17th. Khomeini wanted to remind both groups that a faith with one God, one prophet, and one Qur'an should not split into two warring camps. He declared the period from the 12th to 17th Unity Week.

In early June 1989, Khomeini was in a hospital for an operation to stop some internal bleeding. The operation failed. He died on June 3, and the government announced his death the next day. Every year, Iran observes the June 4 anniversary. It falls on Khordad 14, the day before the celebration of 1963's revolutionary uprising.

Family Affairs

In some years, Iran's national holidays and Islamic holidays bunch up. In 2007, one three-week stretch included Chaharshanbeh Souri, Oil Nationalization Day, Muhammad's birthday, Unity Week, Norooz, the anniversary of Muhammad's death, Islamic Republic Day, Sizdah-Bedar, and smaller holidays honoring the martyrdom of various ancient leaders.

By the time a string of holidays like that is over, Iranian teenagers might be tired of holidays and ready to resume their normal daily routine. But their friends and families may have their own big occasions to celebrate. Births and birthdays, for instance, are happy times when loved ones gather.

The most popular event is probably a wedding. Most Iranian women marry in their early 20s, although the age at marriage is slowly rising. Grooms are usually in their middle 20s.

Iranian weddings generally feature a wedding cloth made of cashmere or another beautiful fabric. On the cloth are items that symbolize a good marriage. For instance, bread is a symbol of riches, sugar stands for a sweet life, and pomegranates mean heaven or paradise. Other items on the cloth might be candlesticks, rice, nuts, eggs, salt, a Qur'an, and a mirror.

The official *aghd*, or exchange of vows, may take place with only the couple and their parents on hand. The vows are often simple. The bride promises to be obedient and faithful. The groom, in turn, promises to be faithful and helpful. Then each of them dips a finger into a bowl of honey, which stands for a sweet life, and feeds it to the other one.

While the wedding ceremony itself

aghd
a-KAD

According to a 2004 government report, the average age of marriage is 26.7 for men and 23.9 for women.

At the end of a traditional wedding celebration, the couple heads for their new home with the bride on horseback, wearing a red veil. The groom walks in front of his new wife.

clothes, and brides make a special effort to have the most elaborate wedding gowns, makeup, and hairstyles. Many brides wear Western gowns, though not necessarily in traditional white.

The male guests may not get much of a chance to see the bride. By Islamic law, men and women celebrate in separate rooms. Still, some weddings include a secret (and sometimes wild) party where men and women can be together.

Some teenagers love weddings. Others are not so thrilled to attend events that can get so lavish and crowded. But no teenager's opinion is going to stop a practice as popular as the Iranian wedding.

The Final Trip

Iranians mourn as intensely as they celebrate. Women in particular sob and wail with great force. This is especially true of elderly or old-fashioned women.

In the first days after a death, mourners gather at the house of the next of kin to weep together and console each other. Many mourners bring food. Traditional foods for this time include halvah, fruit, dates, and nuts. The funeral and burial include a memorial service at a mosque.

A week after the death or funeral, mourners gather again at the grave to weep, pray, and read from the Qur'an. Forty days later, they end the mourning period by repeating the ritual. Every year, on the anniversary of the death, they come back and do it again.

can be small and private, the reception is a much bigger affair. Crowds of guests can number in the hundreds. They celebrate with dancing and other festivities that run long into the night. The elaborate wedding banquet usually includes course after course. A typical banquet might include soup, stew, rice, vegetables, and fruit; lamb, chicken, or other meats; and cookies, cakes and pastries. Many guests wear their finest

Street vendors sell a wide range of products, especially around Norooz, when Iranians buy flowers, plants, and goldfish.

5

Working for a Living

TEENAGE IRANIANS HAVE AMBITIONS LIKE TEEN-AGERS ELSEWHERE. They want to be musicians, artists, athletes, doctors, computer engineers, and other respected professionals.

While they train for those dream jobs, some of them look for work as baby-sitters or food servers. A teen in an upper-income family usually does not have to work. But a family with less money will want its teen offspring to help the family make a living. A son might help out at his father's workplace or look for a job of his own as a food server or retail clerk. A daughter might help her mother keep their household running. Some girls also hunt for outside jobs, but many conservative families frown on girls working outside the home.

Unfortunately for ambitious young Iranians, unemployment has held the country down since the early 1990s. At least 2.5 million people cannot find a job. That is around 11 percent of all Iranians who want to work. (In neighboring Pakistan, the jobless rate is only 6.5 percent.) Experts who survey world unemployment suspect that Iran's real unemployment rate is close to twice that much.

Unemployment is especially high for young Iranians. Most people in their teens and early 20s have little work experience. Many employers refuse to hire them. Young women have the most trouble. The jobless rate for women is at least one and a half times the men's rate. Two-thirds of the nation's college graduates are women, but less than one-quarter are jobholders.

Few experts expect Iran's unemployed masses to find work anytime soon. Even worse, new masses are joining them. More than 12 million Iranians, one-sixth of the entire country, are due to graduate high school or college between 2006 and 2010.

The Big Boss

Who is in charge of jobs and employment? The government. It controls most of Iran's business and trade—up to

Iran's struggle with unemployment has led to high poverty rates. Forty percent of people live below the poverty line.

Money Matters

Most Iranians manage to make a living, but they don't have much money to spare. They see prices rising all around them. Meanwhile the amount of money in their pockets stays small, and high-paying jobs are hard to find.

Iranians have a harder life than people in some neighboring countries, such as Kuwait, Saudi Arabia, and the United Arab Emirates. Still, they're better off than their neighbors in Iraq, Afghanistan, or Turkmenistan.

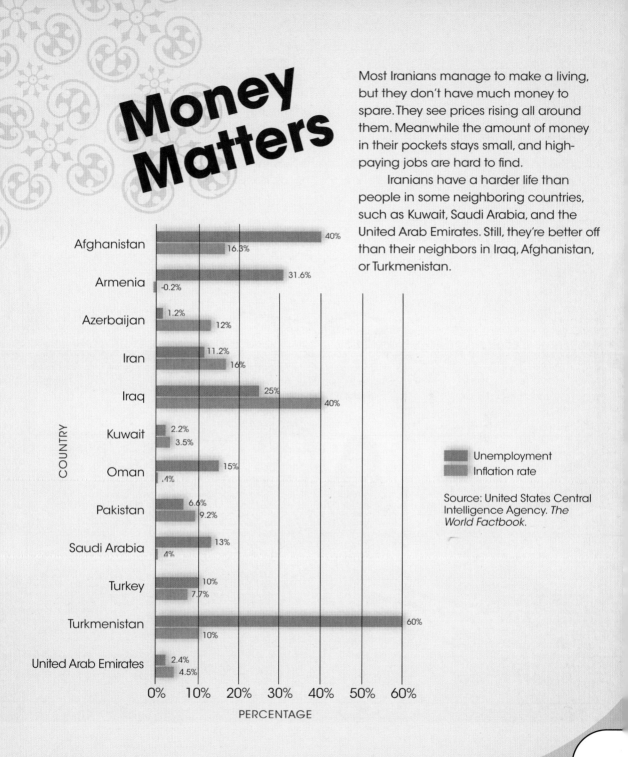

Afghanistan — 40% / 16.3%
Armenia — 31.6% / -0.2%
Azerbaijan — 1.2% / 12%
Iran — 11.2% / 16%
Iraq — 25% / 40%
Kuwait — 2.2% / 3.5%
Oman — 15% / .4%
Pakistan — 6.6% / 9.2%
Saudi Arabia — 13% / 4%
Turkey — 10% / 7.7%
Turkmenistan — 60% / 10%
United Arab Emirates — 2.4% / 4.5%

COUNTRY

PERCENTAGE

Unemployment
Inflation rate

Source: United States Central Intelligence Agency. *The World Factbook.*

80 percent, by some estimates.

The jobholders who earn the most are Shiite clerics. In private conversation, some Iranians call the clerics greedy and corrupt. The clerics who oversee the government, for instance, earn huge fees. Rumors say that some clerics use their political power to acquire money, land, and other valuable items.

Some clerics run *bonyads*.

bonyad
bone-YAAD

The Imam Khomeini Relief Foundation, the largest bonyad in Iran, sponsors a shelter for young women whose families cannot care for them because of drug addiction problems.

A bonyad is a religious and charitable foundation. Ayatollah Khomeini set up the bonyads after he took power in 1979. He used assets from seized lands, bank accounts, and other holdings of the departed shah and his followers. Bonyad Mostazafan, for example, controls businesses ranging from farms to oil wells to hotels. The clerics are to use the profits from the businesses to help the needy or do other good works. Some Iranians believe that the clerics keep the funds for themselves instead.

Not as wealthy as clerics, but nearly as important, are men in uniform. While Iran has the world's 20th-largest population, the country has the eighth-largest military force. About 545,000 troops are on active duty. The military is smaller than the armed forces of China, India, or the United States. But it's larger than the forces of most of Iran's neighbors. What's more, it's bigger than the armed forces of powerful countries such as France and Syria.

The military refuses to take women or girls, but young men may enlist at age 16. They don't have a choice about joining up; eventually, almost every able-bodied male must serve 18 to 24 months. Their enlistment generally starts at age 18. However, some young men with government connections can put it off for months or years. Those who are studying to be clerics need never join at all.

The regular military forces prepare for wars and fight enemy nations. In addition, Iran also has the *pasdaran,* or Revolutionary Guards. Ayatollah Khomeini founded the pasdaran to control forces that might oppose the clerics and their efforts to keep Iran Islamic.

A large part of the pasdaran is the "morality police," or *basij.* This force attacks and jails anyone who opposes the government or disobeys Sharia. Boys too young for the military can join the basij, and girls can join as well. Basij members usually have a powerful devotion to their faith. They feel an urge to ensure that others obey it. The all-volunteer basij numbers anywhere from 90,000 active members and 300,000 reservists to 20 million (the Iranian government's claim). It is not an official department of the government, but the government funds the group and encourages it. After all, one of its former members is President Ahmadinejad.

pasdaran
paas-daa-RAAN

basji
ba-SEEJ

Oil Money

Iran earns more than 80 percent of its money from selling energy, especially oil. The country makes more than

Iranian oil fields produce about 2.5 million barrels of oil a day.

$50 billion per year exporting oil to other countries.

Iran is the world's fourth-largest oil producer, after Saudi Arabia, Russia, and the United States. Most of the oil lies under the western part of the country. Other large deposits sit under northwest Iran, near the Caspian Sea.

Miners, Farmers, Fishermen

Oil and gas exports earn Iran eight times as much money as exports of everything else combined. Still, Iran's other industries create their share of jobs.

Miners dig up metals—for instance, iron and copper in southern and central provinces such as Esfahan, Yazd, and Kerman—and various kinds of stone. Other workers turn them into building materials such as steel and cement. The building industry also benefits from lumbermen who harvest the forests covering parts of the country's northern region near the Elburz Mountains.

Only about one-tenth of Iran's land has enough water or high-quality

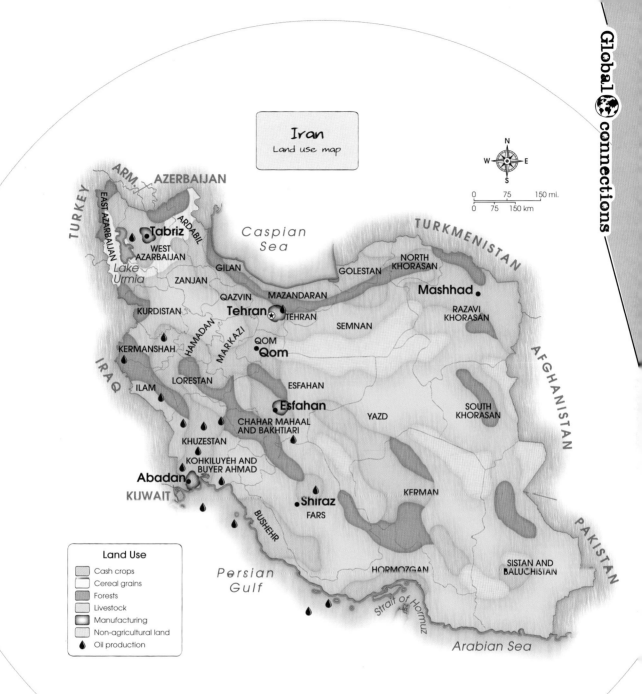

Iran
Land use map

TURKEY

ARM.

AZERBAIJAN

EAST AZARBAIJAN

ARDABIL

• Tabriz

WEST AZARBAIJAN

Lake Urmia

GILAN

ZANJAN

QAZVIN

KURDISTAN

HAMADAN

KERMANSHAH

MARKAZI

LORESTAN

ILAM

IRAQ

KHUZESTAN

KOHKILUYEH AND BUYER AHMAD

Abadan

KUWAIT

BUSHEHR

Caspian Sea

GOLESTAN

NORTH KHORASAN

MAZANDARAN

TURKMENISTAN

Mashhad •

Tehran ⭐ TEHRAN

QOM

• Qom

SEMNAN

RAZAVI KHORASAN

ESFAHAN

Esfahan

CHAHAR MAHAAL AND BAKHTIARI

YAZD

SOUTH KHORASAN

AFGHANISTAN

• Shiraz

FARS

KERMAN

PAKISTAN

Persian Gulf

HORMOZGAN

SISTAN AND BALUCHISTAN

Strait of Hormuz

Arabian Sea

N
W E
S

0   75   150 mi.
0   75   150 km

Land Use

Cash crops
Cereal grains
Forests
Livestock
Manufacturing
Non-agricultural land
◆ Oil production

Division of Labor

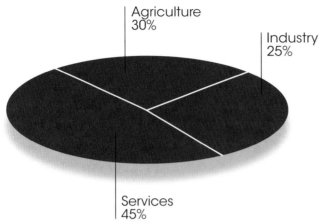

Agriculture
30%

Industry
25%

Services
45%

Source: United States Central Intelligence Agency.
The World Factbook—Iran.

soil for farming. Nonetheless, the food production industry is another big employer. Thirty percent of all employed Iranians raise plants or animals. Many of them grow grains such as rice, wheat, and barley. Others produce dates (particularly in southern provinces such as Khuzestan and Bushehr), oranges, apples, and other fruits. They are both sold in Iran and exported into other countries.

Nuts, particularly pistachios and almonds, are another popular crop. Iranian farmers also plant vegetables such as sugar beets and potatoes, fabrics such as cotton and hemp, and addictive substances such as opium poppies and tobacco.

While farmers raise crops, ranchers raise animals. Like ranchers elsewhere, they sell the milk, meat, and leather hides of cows; the wool and meat of lambs; and the wool and milk of goats. They do not raise pigs, though, because of Islam's rules against contact with swine. Ranching is particularly important in northern provinces such as East Azerbaijan, West Azerbaijan, Lorestan, and North Khorosan. Another northern state, Tehran (home of the famous city), produces much of the country's dairy products, from yogurt to butter to cream.

Fishermen net catfish, kilka (a tiny, anchovylike fish), bream, and sturgeon from the Caspian Sea. Fancy restaurants in dozens of countries serve the sturgeons' eggs. Called caviar, it is an expensive, much-wanted treat.

From the rivers that flow into the Caspian, fishermen gather carp, salmon, and whitefish. Others harvest fish such as tuna in the Gulf of Oman and the Persian Gulf on the country's southern edge.

Hands & Factories

Iran is one of western Asia's leading makers of cars and trucks, shoes and other leather goods, drugs and other chemical products, and electronics (from phones to television equipment to weapons systems). Of all Iranian products, though, the most famous are probably textiles, particularly carpets.

Decorators and collectors around the world love Persian carpets for their complex weaving, elaborate designs, and rich colors. Most Iranian products come from factories, but carpets and other textiles are among the few items that Iranians make by hand.

Iranians don't merely make things. They buy them as well. Although the country has plenty of oil, it has

Iran produces about three-quarters of the world's handmade rugs. Often, more than one crafter will work on the carpets.

few refineries to change the oil into gasoline. It needs to buy gas from other countries. Iranians also import steel, cereal grains, military equipment, machinery such as computers and other electronics, and raw materials to build a variety of products.

Bazaar Days

After Iranians make or import products, they need to get them to customers. The world of retail and services—people waiting on others or selling things to them—makes up nearly half of the non-oil economy. The two account for 47.1 percent of the gross domestic product.

Virtually every big city has a bazaar. The bazaars are huge buildings crowded with tables or stalls. Tehran's Grand Bazaar, for instance, is at least 6 miles (10 km) long. Here thousands of retailers sell everything from carpets to weapons to DVDs. Grocers invite customers to scoop through bins full of spices and nuts. Silver merchants hang shiny tea sets from stands that loom overhead. Clothing salespeople lay out shirts and pants. And everyone—salesperson and customer—haggles over prices.

Many teenagers get their first jobs working for a bazaar merchant. Others,

A Bad Job

Iranian teenage girls by the thousands go into prostitution, selling their bodies for cash. Tehran alone has least 84,000 prostitutes, according to estimates from the Iranian government and University of Rhode Island Women's Studies professor Donna Hughes. The entire nation may have millions.

Many or even most of these young women sell themselves because they need money and cannot find a decent job. Often a young Iranian prostitute comes from a poor family. She may be the only one in her household who makes a living.

Tehran's Grand Bazaar is often referred to as a city within a city.

especially in the big cities, find work in big shopping malls or restaurants. Teahouses are popular places to take a break, and many young Iranians in big cities enjoy fast-food restaurants.

They buy pizza, hamburgers, and fried chicken at places like the restaurant chain Boof, which seems likely to become the McDonald's of Iran.

73

Iranian teens enjoy the slopes, even though the ski police keep close watch to ensure Sharia is followed.

6

Relaxing Under Sharia

TEENS OFTEN ARE QUICK TO NOTICE ANYTHING THAT SEEMS FUN OR ENTERTAINING. But so are Iran's religious leaders. Since they believe God is the provider of all good things, they feel that no one really needs to create entertainment. Under their interpretation of Sharia, people should not distract themselves with activities that give them so much pleasure that they ignore their faith. As a result, Iran's government works hard to regulate the world of Iranian leisure.

Some Iranian teenagers devote themselves to Islam so thoroughly that it satisfies all of their needs. But most Iranian teenagers are not so devout. They like to have a good time. A number of them complain that the country is short on places where teens can have fun. The country has no teen dance clubs or other places where boys can mix with girls.

Instead, teenagers hang around with each other at home, on the streets, or at malls. Shopping is a popular pastime, especially among girls. Iran's shopping malls are as large and extravagant as almost any in the world. The stores sell internationally famous products—nearly everything from LEGOs to Levi's.

When the government began shutting down newspapers, University of Tehran students held protests against the censorship.

Words at War

Reading for fun is a touchy matter under Iran's Islamic government. From 2000 to 2006, the government shut down more than 100 newspapers and magazines. In most cases, the government was angry at them for printing criticism of the government or the religious authorities. The government does allow many other publications to exist, including foreign magazines such as *Time* and *Newsweek*. The Iranian editions, though, go on sale without anything "un-Islamic." This includes images of women in short skirts or cartoons that make fun of Muslim leaders.

Iran's homegrown publications include popular teen magazines featuring celebrity interviews, illustrated with photos. Quite a few teenagers enjoy poetry as well. Virtually every Iranian knows the works of Hafez, a 14th-century mystic who composed love poems. (Iran's religious leaders say that Hafez was revealing his love of Allah.) In one of his most famous works, Hafez regrets leaving his lover behind while he went off to see the world. In a modern interpretation, he ends the poem by telling himself:

By following my own will, I brought my reputation to ruin.
How can our secret [love] remain secret when people assemble to tell of it?
Hafez, if you desire her presence, do not be absent [from her].
When you visit your beloved, abandon the world and let it go.

On the Screen

Like TV networks in other countries, Iran's channels broadcast news, sports, comedies, and other kinds of programs. Soap operas are especially popular.

Iran's television channels run under government control. "The freedom of expression and dissemination [spreading] of thoughts must be guaranteed in keeping with Islamic criteria [rules]," says Article 175 of the country's constitution. In other words, virtually all TV shows send the message that Iranians should follow Islamic principles.

To get other programs, 10 million Iranians own satellite dishes. Iranian teens watch MTV and Persian-language shows, beamed from Los Angeles. (The California city is the home of both Hollywood and more than half a million Iranian-Americans.) Iran's government has started to fight back by taking down the dishes. Every so often trucks clear out entire neighborhoods, sweeping up hundreds of dishes at a time.

In addition to watching television, Iranians love going to the movies. The most popular movies are usually funny ones. The 2006 hit *Cease Fire*, for instance, is a romantic comedy about two bickering newlyweds. Another comedy, 2004's *The Lizard,* is about a thief who disguises himself as a mullah, a Muslim religious leader. It was a success until the authorities called it offensive. They pulled it from the theaters.

Many young Iranians love movies from India, Europe, and the United States, but they can't always see them. In October 2005, the government's Supreme Council of the Cultural Revolution outlawed movies with nonreligious or anti-religious ideas. Also banned were those that promoted equality for females. Despite the ban, many Iranians buy illegal DVDs of Hollywood movies smuggled in from outside the country.

Despite being illegal, satellite dishes cover the roofs of homes in Tehran. Police routinely raid homes to collect the dishes.

Music, Music, Music

Some Islamic scholars disapprove of all music, but Iran's leaders aren't so strict. They allow traditional Iranian music, which depends largely on instruments such as the guitarlike, three-stringed *setar*.

setar
she-TAAR

Many teens prefer Persian pop music, particularly love songs with a strong bass beat. Much of it comes from Iranian exiles such as singer-songwriter Shadmehr Aghili, who lives in Canada. Rappers who slam out lines in Persian are popular, too.

Musicians who sound too much like American or European bands have to be careful, though. In December 2005, the Supreme Council of the Cultural Revolution ordered the nation's radio and television stations to broadcast only music that the council has approved as artistic, such as classical Iranian music. The council banned Western music, which it defined as indecent.

Nevertheless, bootleg CDs of performers from Eric Clapton to Shakira to Eminem have sold well. There's also a huge audience for Metallica and other heavy-metal bands. Headbanging, it seems, is a universal language.

The Playing Field

Iranian teens love sports. Among their favorites are tennis, basketball, volleyball, tennis, and pingpong. As with most other aspects of Iranian life, boys and girls play on separate teams and on separate playing fields.

The most popular sport and the country's national game is football (soccer). Every city has football fields, and teenage Iranians dream of playing professionally. As a Tehran teenager named Abbas Jazzi has said, "I live for my football. It is like medicine for me.

Even when I am sick, if I play I feel so much better." The sport is so popular that Iran has one of the world's biggest football arenas. Tehran's Azadi Stadium seats 100,000 people. When the Iranian national team qualified for the World Cup championships in 2006, young Iranians poured out of their homes. They celebrated in the streets, cheering and honking car horns.

Possibly the second most favorite sport is wrestling. Iranians have a tradition of wrestling that goes back for centuries. Its young wrestlers often score medals in world championships.

Iranians who can afford to travel and buy equipment go skiing, a fact that surprises people who forget that Iran is not a desert country like Iraq or Saudi Arabia. (Only about one-sixth of Iran is desert.) Snow falls every winter on Tehran and the nearby Elburz Mountains. The ski resorts Darbandsar and Shemshak have become famous.

Iranian teenagers take to the hills even in seasons without snow. Hiking is popular, if only because it gets young Iranians away from the always watchful and sometimes violent members of the basij. In the hills, some women remove their head scarves, and young couples can safely hold hands or kiss.

Swimming is popular in the summer, when places such as Tehran can top 100 degrees Fahrenheit (38 degrees Celsius) As usual, men and women must use different swimming pools and different sections of the beaches.

On the Road

Everyone likes a vacation. Iranians who can afford to leave town will visit relatives. Day trips and long weekends are popular. And almost everyone takes some time off during the two weeks between the fire festival Chaharshanbeh Souri and the nature holiday Sizdah-Bedar.

Iranians are known for their generousity toward visitors. They honor their

Villagers watch two young men in a freestyle wrestling match at a traditional wedding party.

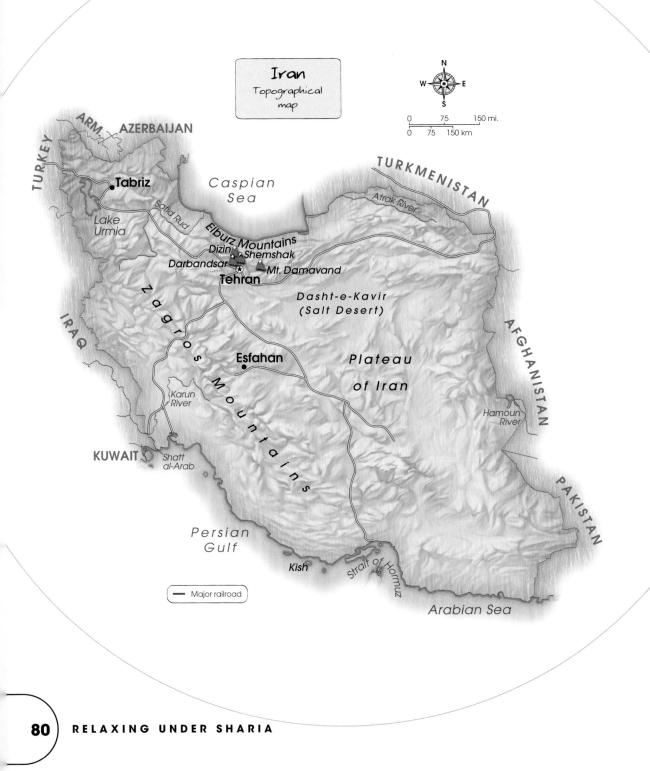

Iran
Topographical
map

N
W   E
S

0   75   150 mi.
0   75   150 km

TURKEY

ARM.

AZERBAIJAN

Tabriz

Caspian
Sea

TURKMENISTAN

Atrak River

Lake
Urmia

Safid Rud

Elburz Mountains

Dizin   Shemshak

Darbandsar

Tehran

Mt. Damavand

Dasht-e-Kavir
(Salt Desert)

AFGHANISTAN

IRAQ

Zagros Mountains

Esfahan

Plateau
of Iran

Karun
River

Hamoun
River

KUWAIT

Shatt
al-Arab

Persian
Gulf

Kish

Strait of Hormuz

PAKISTAN

Arabian Sea

— Major railroad

guests with enormous, elaborate meals. And they always insist guests spend the night or, even better, the week.

In summertime, Iranians head to the water. About one-fourth of the country's northern border is the shore of the Caspian Sea, less than a 150-mile (250-km) drive from Tehran. The shoreline's weather is humid and sometimes rainy but comfortable, like a cool tropical island. The shore is so popular that rich Tehranis keep vacation homes there.

In the Persian Gulf, there is another popular resort area, the island of Kish. Iranians like the island for its warm weather, luxurious hotels, fancy shops, and especially its freedoms. To attract foreign tourists, the government has loosened its rules on Kish. Men and women may hug in public, and women may wear clothes that reveal some skin. At the same time, though, the government divides the beaches into male and female sections, even for visitors who are not devout Muslims. Iran's government says that Kish receives more than a million visitors per year.

Rich Iranians travel beyond Kish and the Caspian. The state-owned Iran Air flies to Europe, the Middle East, and Asia. Some travelers even visit relatives in North America. Iranians who can't afford plane tickets can get around in other ways. Throughout the country, for instance, buses provide a comfortable, if sometimes crowded, ride.

Although it's not really allowed, women on the island of Kish feel comfortable taking off their hejab. They can also bare their arms and roll their jeans up to their calves.

81

Looking Ahead

WHAT IS THE FUTURE FOR IRAN'S TEENAGERS? Some things seem clear. President Ahmadinejad, who has called for stronger enforcement of Islamic law, is scheduled to leave office by the middle of 2009. And in 2010, high school students' grades—and not the dreaded Konkoor—will decide which teenagers go to college.

Other things won't happen on such a firm schedule, but many experts expect changes within the next five to 15 years. Iran depends on its flow of oil to bring in money from other countries. The country's economy is already somewhat sluggish. A problem with the oil supply might slow it down even more.

No matter what happens, though, Iranian teens will find ways to be happy. Iran—where people value both family and visitors—is a country where no one needs to be alone. In addition to family, young people can usually depend on their friends and often on their faith to help them handle everything from the pressures of the Konkoor to the watchful police. Life is not always easy in Iran, but Iranians find ways to keep going.

After all, they have been going strong for about 10,000 years.

At a Glance

Official name: Jomhuri-ye Eslami-ye Iran (Islamic Republic of Iran)

Capital: Tehran

People

Population: 68,688,433

Population by age group:
0–14 years: 26.1%
15–64 years: 69%
65 years and over: 4.9%

Life expectancy at birth: 70.26 years

Official language: Persian

Other common languages: Persian dialects, Turkic and Turkic dialects, Kurdish, Luri, Balochi, Arabic, Turkish

Religions:
Shi'a Islam: 89%
Sunni Islam: 9%
Zoroastrianism, Judaism, Christianity, and Baha'i: 2%

Legal ages
Alcohol consumption: Illegal for all ages
Driver's license: 18
Employment: 15
Leave school: End of eighth grade (usually age 14)
Marriage: 15 (males), 9 (females)
Military service: 16 for volunteers, 18 for draftees (males only)
Voting: 18

Government

Type of government: Theocratic republic

Chief of state: Supreme leader, appointed for life by the Assembly of Experts

Head of government: President, elected by popular vote for four-year term

Lawmaking body: Majlis-e-Shura-ye-Eslami (Islamic Consultative Assembly), elected by popular vote

Administrative divisions: 30 ostanha (provinces)

Independence: April 1, 1979, in a revolution against the royal government of Shah Reza Pahlavi

National flag: The emblem on the Iranian flag resembles a tulip (a flower to honor those who died for their country). The sword represents the nation's strength. The four crescents (which are symbols of Islam) are versions of letters that spell out the word *Allah*.

Geography

Total Area: 636,296 square miles (1.6 million sq km)

Climate: Mostly arid or semiarid; subtropical along Caspian Sea coast

Highest point: Kuh-e (Mount) Damavand, 18,606 feet (5,671 meters)

Lowest point: Caspian Sea, 92 feet (28 m) below sea level

Major rivers: Atrak, Hamoun, Karun, Safid Rud, Urmia

Major landforms: Elburz Mountains, Zagros Mountains, Iranian plateau, Dasht-e Kavir desert

Economy

Currency: Iranian rial

Population below poverty line: 40%

Major natural resources: Petroleum, natural gas, coal, chromium, copper, iron ore, lead, manganese, zinc, sulfur

Major agricultural products: Wheat, rice, other grains, sugar beets, fruits, nuts, cotton, dairy products, wool, caviar

Major exports: Petroleum, chemical and petrochemical products, fruits and nuts, carpets

Major imports: Gasoline, steel, cereal grains, machinery (such as computers and other electronics), industrial raw materials, military equipment

Historical Timeline

The Achaemenid dynasty builds a nation called Persia, which becomes the Persian Empire; in 247 B.C., the Parthian dynasty begins its rule

Mongol armies under Genghis Khan sweep in from the east and conquer Persia

Treaty ends 150 years of war against the Ottoman Empire

Arab armies conquer Persia and introduce a new religion, Islam

c. 8000 B.C.　　**c. 560** B.C.　　**224** A.D.　　**c. 650**　　**c. 1000**　　**1220**　　**1501**　　**1639**

Ismail Safavi declares himself Shah Ismail I and orders the nation to follow his religion, Shia Islam

One of the world's oldest civilizations begins in Iran

Modern Persian language (Farsi) begins to emerge

Sasanian dynasty rules Persia for centuries; Zoroastrianism becomes the accepted religion

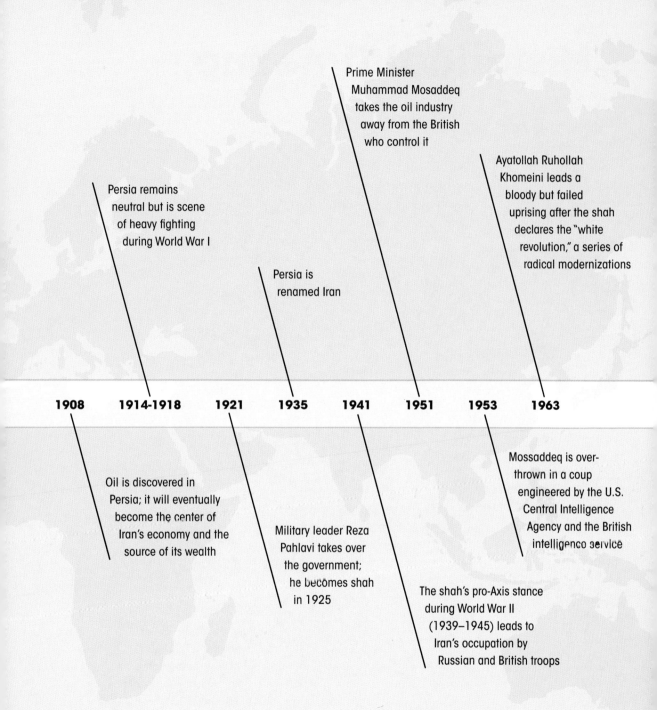

Persia remains
neutral but is scene
of heavy fighting
during World War I

Prime Minister
Muhammad Mosaddeq
takes the oil industry
away from the British
who control it

Ayatollah Ruhollah
Khomeini leads a
bloody but failed
uprising after the shah
declares the "white
revolution," a series of
radical modernizations

Persia is
renamed Iran

1908   **1914–1918**   **1921**   **1935**   **1941**   **1951**   **1953**   **1963**

Oil is discovered in
Persia; it will eventually
become the center of
Iran's economy and the
source of its wealth

Military leader Reza
Pahlavi takes over
the government;
he becomes shah
in 1925

Mossaddeq is over-
thrown in a coup
engineered by the U.S.
Central Intelligence
Agency and the British
intelligence service

The shah's pro-Axis stance
during World War II
(1939–1945) leads to
Iran's occupation by
Russian and British troops

Historical Timeline

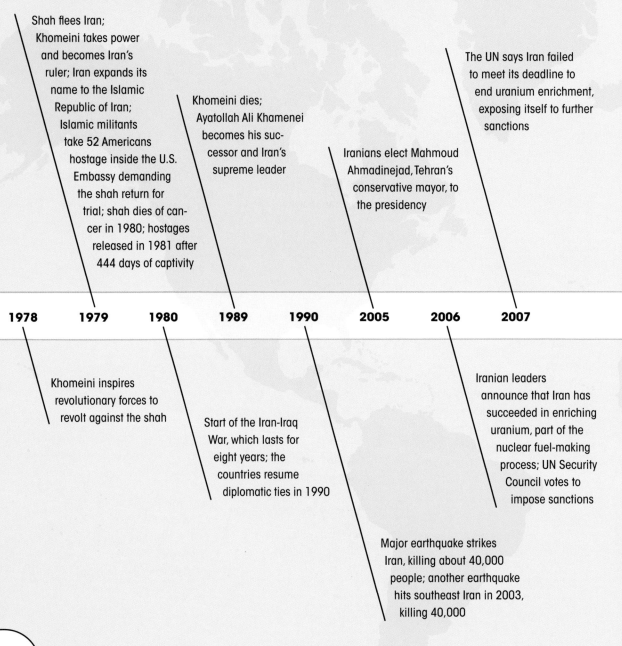

Shah flees Iran; Khomeini takes power and becomes Iran's ruler; Iran expands its name to the Islamic Republic of Iran; Islamic militants take 52 Americans hostage inside the U.S. Embassy demanding the shah return for trial; shah dies of cancer in 1980; hostages released in 1981 after 444 days of captivity

Khomeini dies; Ayatollah Ali Khamenei becomes his successor and Iran's supreme leader

Iranians elect Mahmoud Ahmadinejad, Tehran's conservative mayor, to the presidency

The UN says Iran failed to meet its deadline to end uranium enrichment, exposing itself to further sanctions

1978   1979   1980   1989   1990   2005   2006   2007

Khomeini inspires revolutionary forces to revolt against the shah

Start of the Iran-Iraq War, which lasts for eight years; the countries resume diplomatic ties in 1990

Iranian leaders announce that Iran has succeeded in enriching uranium, part of the nuclear fuel-making process; UN Security Council votes to impose sanctions

Major earthquake strikes Iran, killing about 40,000 people; another earthquake hits southeast Iran in 2003, killing 40,000

Glossary

clerics	religious leaders
gross domestic product	the total value of all goods and services produced in a country during a specific period
hejab	dress code that requires women to cover all skin and hair, except their hands and faces; also a scarf that covers a woman's hair
imam	high-ranking Muslim leader
inflation rate	the amount that prices rise during a certain time period
Islam	Iran's state religion, founded by the prophet Muhammad; followers of Islam are called Muslims
martyrdom	the suffering and death of a person who would rather die than deny his or her religion
mosques	Islamic places of worship
Persian	Iran's main language; also a person from Persia, or a description of anything connected to Persia (which was Iran's name until 1935), such as the Persian Empire
Qur'an	the holy book of Islam, which consists mainly of the revelations that Muhammad received from God during the seventh century
rial	the monetary unit of Iran
Shiites	Muslims who believe that Ali and his descendents were the only rightful guides after the prophet Muhammad
Sunnis	Muslims who believe that the first four Muslim leaders after the prophet Muhammad were rightful guides

Additional Resources

IN THE LIBRARY

Fiction and nonfiction titles to further enhance your introduction to teens in Iran, past and present.

Cook, Jennifer. *An Iranian Mosaic*. Victoria, B.C., Canada: Trafford Publishing, 2006.

Fletcher, Susan. *Shadow Spinner*. New York: Aladdin Books, 1999.

Laird, Elizabeth. *Kiss the Dust*. New York: Puffin, 1994.

Cartlidge, Cherese. *Iran*. San Diego: Lucent Books, 2002.

Greenblatt, Miriam. *Iran*. New York: Children's Press, 2003.

Habeeb, William Mark. *Iran*. Philadelphia: Mason Crest Publishers, 2004.

Kheirabadi, Masoud. *Iran*. Philadelphia: Chelsea House Publishers, 2003.

Kheirabadi, Masoud. *Islam*. Philadelphia: Chelsea House Publishers, 2004.

ON THE WEB

For more information on this topic, use FactHound.

1. Go to www.facthound.com
2. Type in this book ID: 0756533007
3. Click on the *Fetch It* button.

Look for more Global Connections books.

Source Notes

Page 16, column 2, line 1: Sayyid Ali Khamenei. Leader's Address to Young Inventors and Innovators. 19 April 2005. www.khamenei.ir/EN/Speech/detail.jsp?id=20050419A

Page 19, column 2, line 1: Malihe Maghazei. "Iran." *Teen Life in the Middle East.* Ed. Ali Akbar Mahdi. Westport, Conn.: Greenwood Press, 2003, p. 20.

Page 20, column 2, line 6: aytak_83. "How to Stop the Spinning: Comments." Online posting. 12 Aug. 2006. Yahoo! Health. 26 March 2007. http://health.yahoo.com/experts/gabbyguide/84/how-to-stop-the-spinning/comments;_ylt=A jtIEk6NWpq6sIB0cZBu6KqRpM8F?cin=15#comment

Page 24, sidebar, line 4: "Islamic Republic of Iran Constitution." *Iran Online.* 26 March 2007. www.iranonline.com/iran/iran-info/Government/constitution.html

Page 26, column 1, line 10: Alex Bigham. *Voices From Iran.* London: The Foreign Policy Center, 2006, p. 13. http://fpc.org.uk/fsblob/797.pdf

Page 26, column 2, line 11: "View From Iran: Growing Up in Iran." Weblog entry. 27 Aug. 2006. 29 March 2007. http://viewfromiran.blogspot.com/2006/08/growing-up-in-iran.html

Page 27, column 1, line 5: "View From Iran: Millions of Brilliant Liars." Weblog entry. 28 Sept. 2005. 29 March 2007. http://viewfromiran.blogspot.com/2005/09/millions-of-brilliant-liars.html

Page 27, column 2, line 2: "Islamic Penal Code of Iran." Iran Human Rights Documentation Center. 29 March 2007. www.iranhrdc.org/english/pdfs/Codes/ThePenalCode.pdf

Page 32, column 1, line 10: Trans. M.H. Shakir. "The Women." *The Holy Qur'an.* Tahrike Tarsile Qur'an, Inc., 1983. UM Digital Library Production Service. University of Michigan, Ann Arbor, Mich., 7 Jan. 2000. http://quod.lib.umich.edu/cgi/k/koran/koran-idx?type=DIV0&byte=114839

Page 33, column 2, line 10: Trans. M.H. Shakir. "The Clans." *The Holy Qur'an.* Tahrike Tarsile Qur'an, Inc., 1983. UM Digital Library Production Service. University of Michigan, Ann Arbor, Mich., 7 Jan. 2000. http://quod.lib.umich.edu/cgi/k/koran/koran-idx?type=DIV0&byte=650389

Page 35, column 1, line 2: Iranian Girl. "Here I am Again …" Weblog entry. 16 July 2005. 29 March 2007. http://iranian-girl.blogspot.com/2005_07_01_iranian-girl_archive.html

Page 40, column 1, line 3: *Teen Life in the Middle East,* p. 24.

Page 40, column 2, line 9: Iranian Girl. "Finally, I Have a Firm Full-time Job …" Weblog entry. 8 Oct. 2005. 29 March 2007. http://iranian-girl.blogspot.com/2005_10_01_iranian-girl_archive.html

Page 45, column 1, line 1: Brian Murphy. "Iran's Latest Secret Chic: Tattoos." *Seattle Post-Intelligencer.* 10 Aug. 2006. 26 March 2007. http://seattlepi.nwsource.com/lifestyle/280611_iraniantattoos10.html

Page 45, column 2, line 13: Sara Nobari. "Dipped in Silky Water." *Iranian.com.* 21 Sept. 2005. 26 March 2007. www.iranian.com/Travelers/2005/September/Nobari/

Page 46, column 1, line 21: "The Civil Code of the Islamic Republic of Iran." Alvavi & Associates. 8 May 2007. www.alaviandassociates.com/documents/civilcode.pdf

Page 46, column 2, line 1: Tess Strand Alipour. "Iron Chef." Weblog entry. The Superheavy. 26 May 2006. 30 March 2007. www.thesuperheavy.com/permalink/2006/05/26/Iron_Chef.html

Page 49, column 2, line 5: *The Holy Qur'an,* http://quod.lib.umich.edu/cgi/k/koran/koran-idx?type=DIV0&byte=629383

Page 50, column 1, line 7: Proshat the Great. "A Single Woman in Tehran." Weblog entry. 23 Sept. 2006. 30 March 2007. http://proshatthegreat.blogspot.com/2006/09/single-woman-in-tehran.html

Page 76, column 2, line 12: Author's interpretation of various translations at the following: "Hafiz: Versions of One Ode." Spiritual Learning. 30 March 2007. www.spiritual-learning.com/hafiz-compare.html; and "The Poetry of Hafiz of Shiraz." The Songs of Hafiz.com. 30 March 2007. www.thesongsofhafiz.com/hafizpoetry.htm

Page 77, column 1, line 7: "Islamic Republic of Iran Constitution: Article 175." *Iran Online.* 26 March 2007. www.iranonline.com/iran/iran-info/Government/constitution-12.html

Page 78, column 2, line 11: Miranda Eeles. "Abbas Jazzi, 16, Lives for Football in a Tough Neighbourhood in Iran." UNICEF.com. 2006. 30 March 2007. www.unicef.org/football/index_intro_33826.html

Pages 84–85, At a Glance: United States Central Intelligence Agency. *The World Factbook—Iran.* 15 March 2007. 4 April 2007. www.cia.gov/library/publications/the-world-factbook/geos/ir.html

Select Bibliography

Adelkhah, Fariba. *Being Modern in Iran*. New York: Columbia University Press, 2000.

"Country Guides: Iran." *Washington Post*. 2007. 3 April 2007. www.washingtonpost. com/wp-srv/world/countries/iran.html?nav=el

"Country Profile: Iran." *BBC News*. 22 Jan. 2007. 4 April 2007. http://news.bbc.co.uk/1/ hi/world/middle_east/country_profiles/790877.stm

Drew, Paula E. "Iran (Jomhoori-Islam-Iran)." *The Continuum Complete International Encyclopedia of Sexuality*. Ed. Robert T. Francoeur. New York: Continuum Publishing Company, 2004.

Hiro, Dilip. *The Iranian Labyrinth: Journeys through Theocratic Iran and Its Furies*. New York: Nation Books, 2005.

International Monetary Fund. "Islamic Republic of Iran: Statistical Appendix." *IMF Country Report* 7.101, March 2007.

Litvak, Meir. "Iran's Rebellious Youth." *The Middle East: The Impact of Generational Change*. Ed. Asher Susser. Trans. Avi Aronsky. Tel Aviv: Moshe Dayan Center for Middle Eastern and African Studies, Tel Aviv University, 2005.

Maghazci, Malihe. "Iran." *Teen Life in the Middle East*. Ed. Ali Akbar Mahdi. Westport, Conn.: Greenwood Press, 2003.

Mohammadi, Mohammad Reza, and Kazem Mohammad, Farideh K.A. Farahani, Siamak Alikhani, Mohammad Zare, Fahimeh R. Tehrani, Ali Ramezankhani, and Farshid Alaeddini. "Reproductive Knowledge, Attitudes and Behavior Among Adolescent Males in Tehran, Iran." *International Family Planning Perspectives* (March 2006), pp. 35–43.

Price, Massoume. *Iran's Diverse Peoples: A Reference Sourcebook*. Santa Barbara, Calif.: ABC-CLIO, 2005.

United States Library of Congress. Federal Research Division. "Country Profile: Iran." March 2006. http://lcweb2.loc.gov/frd/cs/ profiles/Iran.pdf

World Bank. *2006 World Development Indicators*. Washington, D.C.: The World Bank, 2006.

Index

About the Author
David Seidman

David Seidman has written more than 30 books on subjects ranging from Latino Americans to Spider-Man to the F/A-18 warplane. He has been an editor at the *Los Angeles Times* and Disney Publishing, a novelist, a stand-up comedian, a comic-book writer, and a teacher of writing at UCLA. He lives in West Hollywood, California.

About the Content Adviser
Faegheh Shirazi, Ph.D.

As a professor at the University of Texas at Austin, Faegheh Shirazi teaches a range of courses on Iranian culture and society. In her own research, her main focus is textiles and clothing, particularly the hejab. She also studies issues of women, rituals, and rites of passage in Islamic societies. Dr. Shirazi is the author of *The Veil Unveiled: Hijab in Modern Culture*.

border to border • teen to teen • border to border • teen to teen • border to border